Eton Teashop

Eton Teashop

Peg Hope-Jones

British Broadcasting Corporation

To the evergreen memory of
my dear old partner
Chloe

The BBC *Woman's Hour* serial
first broadcast in September 1978 based on
this book was abridged and produced by
Pat McLoughlin and read by Mary Wimbush

Published by the
British Broadcasting Corporation
35 Marylebone High Street
London WIM 4AA

ISBN 0 563 17499 4

First published 1978
© Peg Hope-Jones 1978

Printed in England
by Butler & Tanner Ltd
Frome and London

Contents

Foreword

I never read forewords myself. I am always too anxious to get on with the book. But in case there are some who do, it would seem churlish not first to thank my long-suffering step-daughter, Susan Hope-Jones, whose grammar far transcends mine.

I rarely go back to Eton now; it is too full of ghosts. Superficially it is much the same as it was when we were there. There still go the Dames (matrons), bustling up and down High Street, and the Beaks (masters), stalking about preoccupied wearing their stiff 'stick-up' collars and white butterfly ties. All the boys are now hatless and appear sprucer than they used to be. But these people might be *our* Dames, *our* Beaks, or *our* boys. They aren't; and there is barely a face there we would recognise or who would recognise us.

Only the River Thames divides Eton from the Royal Borough of Windsor, but in our day the two towns might have been different territories. Windsor, dominated as it is by the Castle, sprawls over places where when young I used to gather wild strawberries. It now possesses housing-estates, bus stations, schools, a theatre and so on. It boasts about twenty-seven thousand souls. Little Eton, which without the College, has a population of about four thousand, cannot expand. Although it once had the effrontery to possess an Urban District Council, it is really more like a village. High Street is bounded at one end by Windsor Bridge and at the other by Eton College itself.

High Street was far more domestic and interesting when Chloe and I inhabited it. Now, many of our friends, the individual grocers, tailors, outfitters and so on have gone, and made way for antique dealers and 'gifte shoppes'. 'Chloe's' itself looks exactly the same from the road, though inside (not before it was needed), it has been gutted from top to bottom and is now the prim habitation of junior bachelor Beaks. I wonder what Mrs Wright the First's ghost thinks of that!

1
How about Helping Miss Chloe?

Chloe always maintained that her 'dear little Muvver' (as she was always referred to) accepted her 'pore ole Dad's' proposal of marriage because his boots didn't smell of blacking. To anyone who did not know Chloe as I did, this story sounds distinctly improbable, but if 'dear little Muvver' resembled her cheerfully inconsequential daughter at all, I myself am not in the least surprised.

Chloe and I first met in the thirties when I, as a callow and enthusiastic doctor's secretary, was asked to enlarge my scope and perform simple electrical treatment on selected patients. I now know that this obsolete bit of equipment was so arranged that I could not possibly have harmed a fly, but in the early days I regarded it with apprehension. Chloe was my first outside patient, though I had tremulously treated a handful of Eton boys for various small complaints.

Viewed for the first time, this stately person with her dark, deep-set eyes, her aquiline nose and her iron grey hair clustering in curls beneath the brim of a huge hat, was sufficient to inspire awe in someone much less meek than I was at that time. I remember I had arrayed myself in an enormous white overall to give me poise for the encounter, and whether it achieved its object or whether with her curious sixth sense she divined my panic, I shall never know. But she treated me from the first with extreme deference and consequently managed to increase my self-respect a little.

As I palpitatingly turned on the current, she looked dreamily at the apparatus and murmured: 'It look-th like an enormouth th-pider, dothn't it, dear?' Her voice was low and musical but she spoke with a marked lisp.

With all its various wires and earths hanging around the condenser, it certainly did look rather like a spider, and I huskily assented, adding that I didn't care much for spiders.

'Oh!' she said, 'I have a pet one at the shop called Eric. He follow-th me about.'

This was the first time, but alas not the last, that I was to hear of Eric. Every spider that I afterwards found in our little teashop was pronounced by my aged partner to be Eric and not to be destroyed or put outside. In fact spider hunts had to be abandoned until she was out of the way. In the winter once I found her balanced over the draining board holding a tumbler of steaming water to a crevice into which Eric had crawled. 'Just to warm him up, dear,' she admitted unrepentently.

On that first occasion, however, I was innocent of her vagaries and we chatted inconsequentially of this and that. Doctor's records and accounts which I should have been attending to downstairs once my patient was settled, were left untouched.

I soon learned not to be scared of this large, handsome, black-eyed lady in the enormous hat. Her undoubtedly imposing exterior did not quite mask her intense sense of fun nor her overwhelming charitableness. She was one of those rare people who, without appearing to flatter, could boost your morale by praising sincerely one's best feature. That afternoon she plumped for my scarlet complexion.

'What a lovely fresh colour you have, dear,' she remarked. 'I was alway-th so pale and fin as a girl. Now I'm gettin' too fat and I'm going to take th-limmin' tea.'

I, slightly embarrassed by such an unashamed personal onslaught, asked if the tea was effective.

'Well,' lisped Chloe twinkling, 'I haven't tried it yet, but it th-mells awful. Thall I bring thome and we'll try it togevver?'

I visualised Dr Attlee finding us swigging her concoctions in his laboratory and possibly denouncing his new secretary as a drug trafficker or worse, so hastily demurred.

'All right,' she agreed, 'I'll bring you some of my fudge instead, and we'll have a go at the tea when you come and see me.'

This was my first indication that after treatment I was ever going to see her again, and I was delighted, for life was a bit dull. Her easygoing gaiety and her unfailing lovingkindness sparked off something in me.

*   *   *   *   *

We met infrequently over the next nine years or so. We both had too much to do. Felma – it was ages before I realised she was 'Thelma'

– helped her unreliably for some time and then disappeared nobody knew where, so Chloe battled along alone concocting her War-time rock buns, shortcakes and so on.

'Vere's nuffin in vem ver th-ould be, dear,' she would warn me. All the same they seemed to taste nicer than anyone else's. Indeed the shortages we endured in the Second World War did produce from all cooks unbelievable feats of ingenuity.

Occasionally I dropped in on Chloe on my way back from work and was welcomed as if I had returned from furthest Siberia. But we were really too preoccupied to get to know each other well. Once I brought in my mother for a cup of tea. This definitely was *not* a success. Much later I discovered there was only three years difference in age between the two of them, but decades divided them in experience and general outlook. It was silly really to introduce them for they were both rather eccentric in their own way, and eccentrics rarely fraternise. My father had died at least twenty-five years earlier, but my mother always attired herself in unrelieved black to her toes, with the suspicion of a widow's veil draping from her hat. She viewed Chloe's sausage-like curls, pearly-grey dress and jade green pinafore with disfavour, and even before there was a hint of Chloe and I joining forces, they were like oil and water and could not mix. In fact, later on, if they had been less well-bred, they might have scratched each other's eyes out!

Contrariwise, Guy, my brother, a Major in the Marines, went down very well indeed. I took him over for coffee when he was on leave from his ship, and in no time at all Chloe was calling him 'ole fing', and Guy was returning courtesies in the way all seamen can. He didn't even complain of Cupid, Chloe's current white cat, shedding its fur all over his immaculate uniform, and on consideration, I think Guy definitely notched me up a peg or two in Chloe's estimation.

During this time too I once met her with an enormously swollen lip distorting her whole face.

'What on earth have you done?' I asked.

'It wath a beathly wathp,' replied Chloe mournfully, lisping worse than ever. 'And I did want to go to the Duke of Connaught-th funeral.'

'Did you know him?' I asked curiously. I knew that she had held a certain position in society in her youth, but had not expected her to have risen to such heights.

9

'Oh no, dear,' she countered, 'but I fink he admired me. My muvver and I used to watch him ridin' in the Row, and he always raised his whip and acknowledged uth.'

I heard later that she did indeed attend his funeral, and the gossips of Windsor discussed exhaustively who this tall, imposing figure swathed in a huge black veil could be, but they never found out. She got swept along with the chief mourners, and the only difficulty she seemed to encounter was extricating herself and disappearing into the crowd.

What had happened to all the money her family unquestionably owned in the past was a mystery. I fancy Chloe's 'pore ole dad' was a little too fond of horseflesh. She once told me that one of the unlikely reasons for her buying the teashop was because the date of its restoration, carved in the stonework by some zealous builder, coincided with the date her father's horse, Brown Bess, won the Good-wood Stakes.

Her mother too was an heiress in her own right, but in those days there was no Married Women's Property Act, so I suppose her fortune went the same way as her 'pore ole dad's'. Also, a little bit of shady mortgaging of expectations on the part of some of her brothers resulted in Chloe and her sisters being left with only a minute income. One of them, 'dear little Ivy', married into the Indian Army. 'Pore old Kate' eked out her patrimony fairly successfully, aided, in later years, by the Old Age Pension. But Chloe, with great spirit and un-commonly little sense, rented a small flat in Hay Hill, Mayfair! By that time she had already been engaged twice. The first time was at the age of seventeen because she was promised a carriage and pair by her admirer. It ended disastrously because he tried to give her a 'very na-th-ty kith, dear' and she threw him over. She was much more shaken by Reggie – a young army officer to whom she was engaged for two years. It came to an end by mutual consent 'becoth I couldn't write letter-th, dear', and as he was posted to India, this was rather an essential part of the courtship. Certainly, if he had possessed the means to wed immediately, the course of Chloe's life would have been quite different.

She moved into Hay Hill just at the beginning of the First World War, when her youngest and nicest brother, Warwick (Woggie to his friends) was a dashing young subaltern at the Front. On his leaves he introduced many other dashing young subalterns, and although well into her thirties by this time, Chloe was constantly in demand.

In spite of being hard-up, she had a way with clothes, and her blue-black hair, huge eyes and fair skin made her an attractive date for any young man. Moreover she was good fun and completely un-demanding. She became a member of the '500 Club' and could always be relied on to produce a male partner for the odd girl.

One would have thought that this full social round would have resulted in a successful marriage and a comfortable old age. Presumably she did not lack offers, but enjoyed having a good time without getting seriously involved. Then there was 'dear old Claud' who was a bit of a mystery to me. He may have been her lover, although I don't think so, for he was much younger than she was, but he remained her faithful and possessive admirer until his death only a few years before Chloe and I met. This may have deterred other suitors; or it may have been, as Chloe was wont to avow, 'We were just old friend-th, dear'.

In later years she insisted on calling our tea-room cat Claudie, which did not strike her as discourteous in the least.

'Claud alway-th thaid hith th-oul would inhabit a cat,' she lisped. 'And really, Claudie has quite a lot of Claud'th way-th.'

We later learned that the Head Master of Eton's christian name was also Claud, which might have led to complications had not Chloe in her inimitable way assured his wife that the naming of our cat was not intended to be disrespectful. The HM's wife, being possessed of one of our rationed plum cakes and also a well-developed sense of humour, remarked that in any case her husband would be honoured to be named after such a handsome animal.

*   *   *   *   *

After ten years even the best jobs are apt to pall, and when I heard that our nicest partner, Dr Attlee, was about to retire, I thought I'd had about enough too.

Mr Kelly, the chemist, and I discussed the situation over a sheaf of boys' prescriptions I had brought in.

'I'm fed up with being secretarial,' I said. 'No responsibility, and constant smoothing ruffled egos.'

'Ye're a resairved occupation where ye are, though,' mused Kelly in his rich Aberdonian. 'They might call ye up!'

This had not occurred to me, as at that time the impact of war-time regulations had not touched me very closely. I would have enjoyed call-up, I think, but by that time my mother, with whom

I lived in Windsor, was old and ailing and it didn't seem fair to abandon her.

'Ye'll have to get into fude,' asserted Kelly. 'They'll let you bide then ... How about helping Miss Chloe?'

In those days, a good many indigent gentlewomen ran small olde worlde teashops – all supposed to be 'little gold mines'. I quail even now to think how much I had to learn.

I hate to admit it, but at that time I considered it might be an easy way of acquiring a teashop and running it singlehanded. But I didn't know then the toughness nor the charm of my prospective partner. I resolved to talk to her about it.

The next Sunday I went to see her in Old Windsor Hospital.

'Hallo, dear,' she wheezed. 'I fort last night that they'd taken me to the basement for treatment and that it consisted of armchair springs attached to the walls comin' out and hittin' me. But they say they didn't. Most unnervin'.'

I pointed out that Old Windsor Hospital, being then mostly a cluster of army huts, didn't have a basement, and that anyway she was back here safe in the ward now. That seemed to calm her a little, but it didn't seem the moment to talk 'teashops' with her.

In spite of her obsession with the armchair springs, she did eventually improve and, urged by former customers, the Vicar found a place for her to convalesce.

'Oh dear! Am I goin' to die?' was all the thanks the poor man got when he came to tell her about it.

'No fear!' he replied smilingly. He had a soft spot for Chloe in spite of her previously assuring him that her brain lacked the bump of religion.

The faded ladies at the convalescent home were rather unprepared for Chloe tottering in heroically though wheezily in her huge black hat, slacks and scarlet jacket. There was some discussion among the directors of the home as to whether she ought to be allowed in to the consecrated dining-hall in this attire. She had no other clothes with her because she had been admitted to hospital in a hurry. Eventually it was agreed that it would be deemed satisfactory if she wore her overcoat at mealtimes together with the blue veil all the other convalescents wore. The others at first looked at her askance, but her unforced gaiety, interest in others and kindness soon won them, and they came to regard her as a rather eccentric mascot. They seemed quite sorry when she eventually went.

'Pore ole fings,' she said to me later, overlooking the fact that many of them were considerably younger than she was.

I decided now was the time to get my future settled.

'She's in her room with two gentlemen visitors,' the nice old nun told me. 'It's really rest time, but she would have been so disappointed if I had sent them away.'

All the convalescents' rooms were named after various virtues – Charity, Faith, Godliness, and so on but Chloe's, most inappropriately, was called Quietude. From within came gusts of laughter.

'Could you hear uth from outhide?' lisped Chloe. 'I'm th-uppothed to be restin'.'

I told them they could be heard a quarter of a mile away.

Her visitors were none other than Kelly and his friend and assistant Paul Shaw. They had brought with them a large bunch of yellow chrysanthemums – no mean feat in the middle of the Second World War.

'Aye, we were just discussing raising funds for a new sun-blind for the wee shop,' chuckled Kelly, muting his voice somewhat. 'Paul had the bright idea of having a collecting box labelled "For the Blind" and money would pour in!'

'I couldn't do vat!' Chloe gasped, mock-horrified. 'We might all be th-truck blind as a punishment.'

'Then you wouldn't need a sun-blind at all,' quipped Paul.

Kelly had a thickset teddy-bear figure, and possessed that indefinable something in his face denoting that when he spoke it would be with a Scots accent. Shaw was much slighter with luminous gooseberry eyes and the look of an intelligent sheep. They had met years before in their first job and had stuck together ever since. Kelly ran the pharmacy side of the business, and Shaw the shop and attached wine store. Chloe – and later I myself – never had kinder nor more considerate neighbours.

'I onth tried to thing in the th-treet wiv a friend,' declared Chloe, reverting to the subject of making money. 'We were abtholutely broke then.'

'How much did you take?' asked Paul.

'Well, nuffin' really. I could only croak anyway, and we fort we th-aw a man we knew, tho we rushed froo a th-ide th-treet and pawned our tea-thpoonth instead,' she chuckled.

I have never been able to tell how much Chloe's unusual diction was real and how much acquired over the years. Probably the lisp was always there, but I think she must have adopted the 'fs' for 'ths' and dropping the 'g' at the ends of words, later. By the time I knew her it had all become so automatic that it was part of her personality. If for the sake of clarity I spell some of her pronunciations 'straight' in this narrative, it must never be imagined that she herself ever deviated from 'Chloe language'.

On this historic occasion she had not yet removed her mealtime veil but, Chloe-like, had arranged it to suit her. One end was bunched into a rosette nestling demurely among the curls over one ear, while the remainder flowed gracefully over her shoulder. Her companion convalescents wore their veils like nursing sisters, and I couldn't help suspecting that Chloe's creation was not quite what the management intended. Nevertheless, it was very becoming.

I thought I would plunge in straightaway. The men knew my intentions anyway, and I thought I might need allies.

'Chloe,' I said, 'would you like me as a partner?'

'Yeth, dear,' replied Chloe instantly.

I was so taken aback that I thought she hadn't heard. Even then she was beginning to be a little deaf.

'Are you sure?' I gasped more distinctly. 'I can't cook, you know.'

'That's all right dear. I'll teach you,' she replied.

So that was how I joined the firm.

'Aye: I knew she'd have ye,' grinned Kelly.

2
From Doctors to Doughnuts

All the family, with the astonishing exception of my mother, thought I had gone mad. In spite of her inbuilt antipathy to Chloe, Ma declared: 'Well! You're grown-up now and must do what you like. You always were obstinate like your father. But don't expect me to keep you.'

Friends, knowing my inability to cook, ragged me unmercifully saying I had made an unholy alliance with the new practice of doctors to poison Chloe's customers so that they could amass new patients. Thinking I knew Chloe's happy-go-lucky ways, I decided to get a few lessons in Basic Cookery from a technical college before we joined forces. This was my first mistake in the uphill struggle to become a teashop lady. It would have been difficult for the Government of that time actually to forbid cookery lessons, because of those who for the first time in their lives were left without help – and because of young army wives too. But the microscopic amount of ingredients we were allowed to work with gave me no idea of how, for instance, to turn out a batch of buns at Chloe's. Likewise cake at the technical college in that era was treated as almost a dirty word, since all the emphasis was on how to expand a quarter of a pound of offal to feed a family of six.

A month or two later I was ringing and hammering at the shop door. I had reckoned that in order to be ready with coffee and for early morning shoppers I ought to arrive about half-past eight. Of course on reflection I ought to have checked with Chloe, but in those days I thought I knew it all.

'If you're wanting Miss Chloe, she don't get up until ten o'clock,' volunteered fat Rosie passing hurriedly by on her way to open up the milk shop.

I gasped! The place was supposed to be open by half-past ten! Rosie must have been joking.

By nine o'clock I was beginning to believe her, and looked hopelessly around. Shutters had been removed along the street. Frontages had been swept and steps cleaned – all except Chloe's, which with the new blind tightly pulled down, looked resolutely closed.

Suddenly Mrs Johns appeared. She was the bank manager's wife from next door. 'Are you trying to get in?' she asked superfluously. 'I've got a key.'

This she magically produced from her handbag before bustling off with her shopping basket. It later transpired that all High Street was peppered with Chloe's keys, ever since the fire brigade had to be called to climb in at the first-floor window when Chloe had shut herself out.

Of course I had been in the little place before, but never without its guiding spirit, and not much beyond the tea-room. I suspect now that she used to have a bit of a whisk round before I came anyway. The tiny tea-room boasted five polished tables which at a pinch held four people each. Copper kitchen utensils glowed on the mantelshelf, and the walls were hung with a curious assortment of oil paintings in gilt frames.

'My dear old bruvver used to collect 'em from auctions,' she told me later. This apparently had become such an obsession with him that his wife rebelled, and Chloe undertook to house some of the overflow. An artistic friend of Chloe's had helped her move in, and had had the picture rail lowered to make the room look more 'cottagey', and what with the cretonne curtains and cushions, the flowers on the tables, and the copper, the little place looked glowing and homely – if slightly crumby – as I entered.

If she had searched diligently – which she hadn't – I don't think Chloe could have found more inconvenient premises. She took them firstly because the rent was reasonable, but principally she said because of the good solid and comparatively modern wood block floors which took her fancy. As things turned out, this was not as idiotic as it appeared, for in the floods of 1948 this was about the only house in the street whose floor remained firmly intact. It was a tall house, forty-three stairs from top to bottom, boasting two rooms on each floor except the ground floor, where the long narrow kitchen was built on, and which led on to a horrid yard with no exit. Thus everything – but *everything* – coal, stores, dustbins and so on had to be carried through the tea-room, through a narrow door with a step to the 'middle room' and through another door into the kitchen.

Chloe displayed the home-made cakes in the middle room, from where the staircase led to the other floors. It possessed one pitch-dark larder and a small window looking on to the high wall of the back-yard.

I could just distinguish a tottering pile of wire cooling trays, a butlers' tray, a huge desk, a large, old-fashioned radio and, as I became more accustomed to the gloom, tins, boxes, pots, magazines, and a dilapidated basket chair. As I haltingly groped my way through to the kitchen, I found to my joy an electric light switch – the one in the middle room hadn't worked – and the kitchen was flooded with light. I choked: chaos reigned supreme! The hideous yellow sink at the back was piled high with a conglomerate jumble of pud-ding basins, saucepans, sieves, egg-beaters, plates, saucers, tea cups. On the floor were scattered spoons, knives, sprinklers, lids and other litter. The working table was a clutter of bags of flour, sugar, peel, dried egg, sultanas, all spilling out of their respective containers, some on to the floor. On the fairly capacious gas stove stood an aged enamel jug, carefully covered with a saucer containing a noxious-looking liquid from which I recoiled.

The question of the moment was what to do next. After my mini-scule training I was afraid of baking, and like so many of my genera-tion I had been forcibly kept away from the kitchen in case I upset our old servant. I suppose I could have called Chloe, but I was not yet on those sort of terms with her. After hasty deliberation I decided that getting the tea-room to rights would be first priority, after which I would make a beginning on the washing-up. So I swept the floor, polished the tables and lit the fire, and was just trying to stack the crocks on one side of the sink so that I would have room to drain them on the other, when Chloe materialised.

'Hello, dear,' she beamed. She looked immaculate, her iron-grey curls exactly right, her clover-coloured cardigan and frilly little apron exactly matching.

'You shouldn't be doin' all *vat*,' she objected.

'Well, I've done the fire, and as you know, I'm not yet able to get on with the cooking,' I said.

'Oh, vat's all right,' Chloe replied, who by that time was spreading clean greaseproof paper on to the middle room table, having first switched on a rose-pink reading lamp which I hadn't noticed. She then dived into the dark recesses of the room and produced tin upon tin of home-made cakes, sponges, flapjacks, rock cakes, jam tarts and biscuits. These she arranged daintily on her table and put a plate or two in the window, just to lure in the odd passer-by.

'I finished vese at free this mornin!' she announced happily. 'Have you made the coffee, dear? No, of course you haven't. It'th in that enamel jug. It only wants th-immering.'

At that precise moment all the lights went out.

'Oh dear!' wailed Chloe, a shadowy tragedy queen. 'That beathly meter! I do wish Hevver would come. He usually fixes it for me. I don't fink there's a shilling in the till. We put in the franc that some-times works the thing last week. Where *is* Hevver. No dear, don't try anyfing till Hevver shows you. It's rarver tricky and sometimes get stuck. We'll open up, shall we?'

Luckily 'Hevver' was our first customer. With the alacrity borne of long custom, he produced a shilling from his pocket, dropped on all fours and squirmed under the staging of the front window. Here, by what can only be called sleight of hand he inserted the coin in the meter slot. He then rose smilingly, dusted his trousers, and crossed to warm his backside by the fire.

'Hevver' turned out to be Howard Hetherington – 'Hether' to his friends – a good-looking man in early middle age with velvety eyes. He had the reputation of being a bit of a lad with the girls, in spite of an attractive and devoted wife somewhere in Windsor. But he never got up to anything at Chloe's, and as has been shown was a most useful member of our variegated crew. It took me a very long time to master that meter, and even then I had to take a torch with me.

'Ridiculous place to put the horrid fing,' complained Chloe. 'Peg, dear, would you give Hevver fourpence from the till?'

I was distinctly mystified by this transaction, but it eventually dawned on me that we were repaying him for the shilling he lent us, less the cost of the coffee Chloe was brewing for him and two cakes. This was the way Chloe had always managed her finances. She told me later that the income tax man had once come to see her, but had departed defeated and never come again.

'He said it wasn't wurf the bovver,' she said.

It may have been that she plied him with coffee and cakes. Flag-sellers, encyclopaedia travellers, Sisters of Mercy, always received hospitality at her hands. 'The poor fings are worse off than we are,' she would say.

Much later on I had to take her in hand about the income tax returns.

'*You* might be able to get away with it,' I pronounced forcibly, 'because you are old and ill, but probably they'd put me behind bars and then where should we be?'

'I could come and feed you wiv bun-th,' she chuckled, unmoved.

'That's the zoo, not prison,' I objected tetchily. 'Visitors to prison can only talk through that sort of mesh there is in meatsafes.'

'Oh!' she relented unwillingly. 'I suppose you'd better do somefing about it then, but what a bore . . . Have you ever been to prison, dear? You seem to know an awful lot about it.'

I assured her that so far my record was clean.

*   *   *   *   *

For most of my first morning I tried to retreat to the recesses of the kitchen. Used coffee cups were now being added to the mountains of crockery. I had been only an average sort of secretary, but at least I knew then what I was meant to be doing. Now, I felt embarrassed at meeting the customers, some of them old patients from my former job.

Chloe eventually dug me out. 'Come on, dear,' she urged. 'Vey all want to meet you.'

The first person I encountered was nice Mrs Graham-Campbell, utterly unassuming, but with a formidable pedigree. She was a house-master's wife, and years ago we had forged a link when her toddler had chewed off and swallowed his coat button. No doctor being at hand (they never seemed to be so when wanted), I turned on my soothing act and told her that as the button wasn't scratchy, with a little judicious dose of medicinal paraffin, it would probably emerge without trouble. And so it did, cotton and all, much to our mutual satisfaction. In the dim middle room we greeted each other with cordiality, and I felt our meeting was a good omen. However, our pleasant chat was curtailed by gong-like reverberations coming presumably from our yard.

'Oh dear!' wailed Chloe. 'We've forgotten Mr John-th again! He's the bank manager next door,' she explained, 'and he can't leave the th-trong room to come in here. He beat-th vat awful tin tray when we forget him. Just pass this coffee over the wall, dear, and tell him how th-orry we are.' This I accomplished fairly efficiently, I think, and thus by degrees got accepted into the fold.

Soon I began to realise that our coffee customers came in three different waves: first the more affluent office workers, like Hether and his friends, Nicky the garage proprietor, and Reg the coach impresario, who could all briefly leave a clerk in charge, and who usually cleared off early. Then came the College wives and Dames, and lastly, after a decent interval, the boys.

'The boys will soon be here!' proclaimed Chloe joyfully, when I got back. She was gliding about putting a top-dressing of orderliness to the chaos. In spite of feet misshapen almost to the point of deformity, she managed to retain the movements of a dancer.

Let it not be imagined that the whole of Eton College now descended on our tiny establishment. They had their own tuck-shop, Rowlands, within the precincts, and there were various other shops on the way to our place that catered for them. But I think at that time we were the only firm who made home-made cakes on the premises, and we liked to think that the most discerning came to us.

They were a jolly, motley crew. In 1940 they had not yet bowed to the inevitable and discarded top-hats. But there weren't enough hatters to keep the hats in proper repair. Likewise, most of the younger tailors were in the army, and ankles and even shins often showed below the regulation striped trousers before they could be lengthened. As anyone who has had anything to do with growth of the adolescent young will recognise, it was quite impossible for those old tailors left behind to keep pace. The material of which the boys' uniform is made is by no means warm. Even the 'tails' of the older boys did not compensate for a good flannel suit, and in those days the small boys, measuring under five feet, were condemned to Eton jackets – bum freezers, in the vernacular – and often looked perished with cold. It is small wonder that the authorities appeared to turn a blind eye to a not too conspicuous pullover worn under the regulation waistcoat. So the boys usually turned up arrayed in trousers that were too short, a cotton shirt, a black waistcoat around which showed the edges of, say, a blue pullover, and wrists showing where their fur gloves would not meet their abbreviated sleeves. Outside in the street all this was surmounted by a battered top-hat. The whole effect was rather ludicrous – not that we didn't all look a bit of a mess in those days of clothes rationing.

I have never known what top-hats are made of: could it be rabbit skins? At all events, during the war, the material was unobtainable, and this remarkable headgear soon began to be phased out. Bum-freezers too have now been discontinued, but cotton shirts, striped trousers, waistcoats and tail coats are to this day the accepted school uniform. Of course when the boys play games they get into ordinary sports gear, but woe betide him who is spotted by a Beak or senior boy wearing 'change' in Eton High Street. I don't quite know what happens now, but in our day if sports things were covered by an over-coat, and a top-hat worn, this counted as being suitably attired for the town. Then you weren't fined half-a-crown, which was quite a lot of pocket money in those days, even for the opulent. For several years Chloe kept an elderly top-hat and an ownerless coat in the larder for lending to boys who had come without them, but in the end some wicked wretch never returned them.

However, these sartorial eccentricities didn't diminish the boys' appetites in the least. They had approximately half an hour between 'schools' ending and 'boys' dinner', and usually the whole of our stocks disappeared in that time. I suppose they then went off and ate a hearty lunch! A few had the forethought to bring cake tins – there being no paper bags in those days – and bore a selection of cakes away for 'messing' (tea), but most of them were content to stuff on the premises.

A deathly hush descended when they went. Chloe, humming a little tune, surveyed the disorder with a practised eye.

'We'll soon clear this up after lunch, dear. I'm goin' to rest and take mine up wiv me.'

She gave me a key and I cycled to Windsor to the peace and quiet of my mother's little home.

In the afternoon the tempo definitely slackened. (Indeed, when I had mastered the mysteries of cake-making, I found I could cope with that and customers, and I rarely saw my partner until after teas were over.)

I found on that first day that cooking was not so difficult as I had anticipated as recipes had perforce to be very simple, and Chloe turned out to be a surprisingly good and patient teacher. Learning its in-tricacies, as I did, so late in life, I never quite got over the wonder of putting what looked like a porridge-y mess ('dog-th dinner', Chloe called it) in the oven which in an hour or two would reveal itself as a succulent cake. To the end of our time together she was always a better and more resourceful cook than I, though I somehow got by. It later transpired that she had been a kind of au pair-cum-cookery student in an English teashop in Bruges, which accounted for her care-ful weighing, and her emphasis on getting a set number of cakes from a set amount of dough.

In truth the only real difficulty I had was translating Chloe's vocabulary into plain English. 'I can't find the dancin' lady anywhere,' she would complain. 'I know I had it yesterday.'

In this instance she would be referring to a species of spring-y egg-beater supposed to act magically upon dried eggs. If you gave it a little push along an inclined pastry board it would hop, much to Claudie's mystification and delight, and this, naturally, was how it acquired its name. All Chloe's names were logical really, but one needed to become accustomed to them. The 'flapper' was the most pliable palette knife, 'Old Benbow' was the bendy knife which scratched the last vestige of material from pots and pans, and so on.

On my first afternoon she showed me how to make a batch of scones. Innocently I had always visualised Chloe flinging such ingredients as she happened to possess into the basin with gay abandon, but this was far from the case.

'Here's the proper amount of sour milk,' she pronounced. 'Just slosh it in, and don't handle the dough too much.'

The quantity seemed colossal to me after the sparseness of the technical college materials. 'No: you show me how,' I hastily demurred.

'I fort they'd shown you how to do vem at vat place,' she retorted. She had disapproved heartily of my going there.

'Yes, they did: but you do it first,' I wheedled.

'Oh, all right, dear,' she relented. 'It all must seem very strange to you.'

On these initial afternoons I also picked up some useful wrinkles, some of which I follow to this day.

'Alway-th beware of chocolate cakes in shops you don't know,' was one of her adages. Apparently the strong taste of cocoa can mask a multitude of inadequacies such as rancid fat, and the colour can hide dirty ingredients.

'Alway-th when drinking from a tea-room cup, hold the handle in your left hand, dear,' was another of her doctrines I still follow. I know from experience how sketchily washing-up had to be done, though I suppose the modern washing-up machine is now more widely used and more hygienic.

I also learnt from observation rather than precept how much better it was to wash-up as much as possible as you went along, thus partially avoiding the mad disorder of the morning.

Chloe showed me too how to 'diddle up' yesterday's scones. The trick was to sweep them momentarily under the cold water tap, bundle them into a paper bag and put the bag for a few minutes into a roaringly hot oven. No one seemed to notice the difference, though this device doesn't work with really stale scones.

'It's one of the most useful fings I've learned,' declared Chloe when she showed me what to do. 'I fink I'd have turned into a th'cone otherwise, or more like a cottage loaf, gobblin' up vose damn fings so as not to waste them.'

She also let me into the secret of the contents of the noxious enamel jug I had so nearly thrown away on my first morning. This was the famous Chloe-coffee. It was made by steeping ground coffee in cold water overnight and slowly simmering it in the morning. A quarter of a pound of coffee made fifteen to twenty cups, and was really very potent. Not requiring twenty cups in my present small household, I don't know if it still works or whether the coffee we bought wholesale from the traveller lent itself to this odd procedure.

Mostly the 'tea-bods', as we irreverently called them, were strangers who came to take a peek at one of England's oldest seats of learning. We did have a few old faithfuls from time to time, however. These included cheerful old Miss Wells from the school upholsterer's shop which still exists nearer the school. She, poor dear, suffered from an incurable blood disease, though it didn't seem to get her down. As the years went by she got thinner and thinner, and her good features sharper and sharper so that she began to look like a fairytale witch. She always carried a huge umbrella, and it only needed a little Chloe-imagination to visualise her sailing down to the teashop on it.

Occasionally Hengist and Horsa, as the boys called them, the College physiotherapists, came for tea, but never together. They were sisters, but outside working hours seemed sensibly to lead separate lives. They were stern disciplinarians and Chloe and I were a bit intimidated by them. Once I heard one of them (I forget which) haranguing a meek little Finn sitting at the next table on the subject of Roman Baths. The fall of the Roman Empire she maintained began with the predilection of Romans for lolling about in hot water. When *she* had a bath she always washed standing up. The little Finn appeared cowed and impressed, though I'm sure he had a good wallow when he got back to his hotel that night!

Afternoon customers were served with a pot of tea, two scones, butter, jam and two cakes from a selection of six, at two shillings a crack. How on earth we ever made any money I can't think. After they had gone on that first day I was further initiated into the mysteries of cake-making until late in the evening I returned home exhausted but exhilarated.

Of course I made the most ghastly mistakes at first. The worst one I think was leaving a newly-baked cake on the piano stool which stood opposite the oven. This seat was Chloe's special property, given to her by the dentist's wife. On it she could swivel from the corner of the kitchen table, where she worked, to opposite the oven where she baked, without having to get up – a most useful and intelligent gift which now has pride of place in our sitting-room. On this occasion I was just too late to stop her settling down on my hot cake temporarily resting there on its cooling tray. Minor pandemonium ensued for a minute or two, followed by much lamentation on my part concerning the irreplaceable loss of valuable ingredients, and my general ham-handedness.

'Well, dear,' comforted Chloe with finality, 'everyone does silly things sometimes. It's certainly done somefing good. I've got a warm backside for the first time today.'

Another of my boobs turned out less disastrously. I had been shown by then how to make a sponge mixture in a large flat tin so that it could later be cut into fingers and iced. As I took it from the oven it didn't seem to look quite as it should, and it was only then I realised that I had forgotten to put the sugar into it. Shamefacedly I confessed, thinking of the butter and egg I had wasted.

Chloe was quite unperturbed. 'Vat's all right, dear,' she said. 'We'll have to make it into somefing savoury.'

It is difficult to imagine in these days of plenty how extraordinarily difficult it was to make rationed food – wholesome though it was – taste interesting. Such items as, say, Oxo cubes were as scarce as gold dust, and you had practically to kneel to your greengrocer for the privilege of buying an onion from him.

With the help of a torch, Chloe and I explored the dark larder, and extracted an interesting and varied array of half-empty bottles, tins and jars. Never let it be imagined that any of these things were bad, but they certainly bore unmistakable marks of ancient vintage. As a basis we mixed ground rice and semolina together and cooked it with heaps of pepper and salt. It tasted very nasty indeed. We then added mustard which made the mixture look awful as well.

'It tastes like hot-water-bottles, dear,' pronounced Chloe, scattering in a few herbs and the remains of a bottle of ketchup. This improved it a little, but the whole thing lacked bite. We then went a bit mad and hurled in anything likely to add piquancy. A curious pink concoction resulted, which tasted distinctly unusual to say the least. While Chloe cut the offending sponge into squares, spreading the mixture daintily and decorating it with parsley culled from the backyard, I manufactured a splendid notice:

SAVOURY SLICES (unrationed) PRICE 4d. each.

Kelly came in just as we had finished. It was after closing time, and he came, as he often did, for a natter and to open an obstinately nailed case of dried fruit for us.

'Brrranching out, I see,' he remarked in his rich Scots, as he viewed our handiwork.

'Well, not exactly,' burbled Chloe, her eyes dancing. 'Just an exthperiment ... try a piece?'

'Only if you'll have some as well,' replied our canny Scot, unable to understand our mirth.

So we all had a piece, washed down with the hotted-up remains of the morning coffee, and it really wasn't too bad. We then confessed what had been going on, and good old 'Ed', as he preferred to be called out of working hours, joined in the joke and purchased a piece for Paul, busy bottling and labelling his wines across the road.

'Aye!' he chuckled. 'If we're going to die of eating it, the four of us had better go together.'

But no one did take ill, and in fact customers asked for repeat orders. As we hadn't the faintest idea by that time what had gone into our savoury, we sadly told them – with some truth – that we were unable to obtain the necessary ingredients! In any case, we had already decided that the place was too small for confectionery and savouries.

'Imagine what would happen if an onion or somefing got into a cake,' reflected Chloe. 'We'd lose all our customers!'

3
They called us a Gossip Shop

Chloe had a curious 'mystique' with men. From being an impressive, elegant, rather dignified old lady, she seemed at will to be able to transform herself into a poor bereft maiden left to battle alone with the wicked world. She had but to raise her eyes mournfully to the ceiling and wail, 'I don't know *what* we are going to do', for men to rush to her aid. This gift she exploited to the full, especially on our first contingent of coffee drinkers, and it seldom failed. Thus snow, when it fell, was willingly swept from our pavement, new hooks for the dresser were dropped into her lap, part of a ceiling was re-plastered and coal brought in from our beastly backyard. Coloured china was almost impossible to obtain in those days of austerity, yet the teashop never ran out, and any little job such as oiling squeaky doors or mending a bolt was attended to with alacrity.

Chloe showed no shame about this ability. Indeed I think she was hardly aware of it. 'Vey like doin' it, dear,' she averred.

Needless to say I – not possessing such a talent – kept well out of sight during these transactions. But I don't know where we should have been without our volunteer army.

Women helped us as well, of course, but this didn't seem to me so unusual. Looking back, it seems quite extraordinary that they did so, for a good many of them had husbands to feed and large houses to maintain with little or no staff. In part it was probably because all women like playing shops, and trying to straighten us up was the next best thing. The fact remains that Dames, and the nicest of the Beaks' wives, helped us enormously in our rush hours, serving our coffee, selling our cakes and washing-up. Once, while I was away, Mrs Streatfeild, a house-master's wife, scrubbed the kitchen floor!

On the Fourth of June (Eton's great day), and on other large social occasions, we were obliged to employ labour, mostly because our volunteers were otherwise occupied. We hated this, partly because we had to tidy up, but principally because we had to give orders which undermined the crazy, insouciant atmosphere of the place. Later on, when Chloe became older and iller, and I perforce busier, sunny little Mrs Slatter did come and help 'fettle' us up, as she put it. She was an old friend, for she had been the doctor's cook. In the past I had listened fascinated to her tales of the 'big 'ouses' in which she had operated – like Margaret Powell's *Below Stairs* only more so. At any rate she came before opening time and disappeared with the first customer. She had never worked for Trade before, and in her delightful way was just as snobbish as my mother, who found it almost indefensible that her daughter had become a 'shop-girl' as opposed to being a 'type-writer' – my mother's word for secretary.

*   *   *   *   *

The Dames who came in to drink Chloe's coffee in the morning were not veritable Dames in the old sense of the word. In effect they were merely hard-worked matrons, but the old name stuck. Up to about 1900 Dames were exclusively in charge of boys' boarding houses, but after that the practice was discontinued, and as they died or retired a House-master as well as a Dame were installed. Those boys who were in houses and supervised by Dames and House beaks were called 'Oppidans' as opposed to the seventy talented 'Collegers' who lived in the old part of the college and got into the school by reason of their scholarship. Nowadays Collegers have to pay fees too, but the Foundation, as it is called, dating from the time of Henry VI, provided that the College should be for poor boys. Over the usual uniform they are obliged to wear, during school, black gowns which during the war took on a greenish antique hue, but there didn't seem to be any other difference between them and the Oppidans.

Chloe and I felt sorry for the Dames. Barring a few old battle-axes, they were ladies, hard-up like ourselves, and nobly trying to keep up standards under war-time conditions. Food was restricted, boys' appetites were insatiable, and staff, because of the call-up, were either ridiculously old or ridiculously young. Management of boys' houses varied, of course, depending on whether the house beaks were married or single, but in the majority of cases, Dames were responsible for the catering, the accounts, the health of everyone in the house – about fifty in all – the linen, and above all the boys. Today there is a centrally run catering system I believe, which should relieve the

Dames a little, but even so there is more than enough for them to do.

Moreover they led, in those days, an almost sequestered life. Matrons in most schools are accepted members of a staff room: not so at Eton. There just wasn't a staff room for them, and with a few notable exceptions Beaks and Beaks' wives did not fraternise with them. This, as much as anything else, was because the distance between boys' houses was fairly formidable for a busy person, so it was small wonder that they congregated at Chloe's, using us as a kind of unofficial club. Here they did sometimes encounter Beaks' wives and occasionally struck up friendships with them. But on the whole the gallant little conclave of some twenty-five souls formed a compact group.

Our detractors called us a gossip shop, and to be fair I suppose it was: but it was never malicious gossip, and in many ways it acted as a catharsis for Dames who might otherwise have gone clean off their heads. They would penetrate into the shadowy middle room, pick their way delicately among dimly distinguishable objects, and stand uncomfortably drinking coffee and airing their grievances to their colleagues or to Chloe and me in the kitchen if nobody else happened to be there. They knew we wouldn't make mischief.

Such topics as the menopausal rages of the cook, the honesty or otherwise of the odd man, the impossibility of keeping track of the laundry, and ways of stretching the rations, were discussed with gusto. Sometimes we heard of dramatic incidents such as the time when two boys collided in the corridor. Two doctors had to be sent for, one to staunch bleeding from the jaw of one boy and the other to extract a tooth embedded in the forehead of the opposite victim.

Hearing of this caused me to wonder how my successor at the doctors' had fared. You pretty well had to be a mind reader to be able to find the doctors in an emergency, and Ellen, the parlourmaid, and I had developed an intricate system of discovering where they had deviated from the routine visiting lists they left behind. Not for us the pocket 'bleeper' that some doctors nowadays possess. When it bleeps the doctor merely telephones the medical centre for instructions: but I suppose in those days it would have interfered with aircraft detection – even if it had been invented. Anyway, Betty, the new secretary, was not yet nearly as natty as I had been in tracking the doctors down!

*　　*　　*　　*　　*

Early in our partnership I innocently asked if we couldn't have a little more light in the middle room.

'Well,' replied Chloe dubiously, 'of course it's difficult for you dear, as you don't know where the fings are. We could have the ceiling light mended I suppose, but I fink you'll be th-orry.'

I was: very 'th-orry'.

Nothing was straightforward in that benighted house. I had a fruit-less search for a fuse-box: there wasn't one. Then one of the vanguard coffee drinkers, Reg Try, the coach owner, I think it was, suggested that the fuse probably lived above the light itself in a rose over the flex. And so it proved to be. Each light had its own fuse, and it was a tricky business repairing them. Only one semi-retired electrician in Eton understood the intricacies of the system and even so brought down a lot of plaster from around the ceiling rose every time a fuse required renewing. He also pointed out that all the superannuated electric cable was seated in wood, which was Against the Law, and that at any minute we might go up in flames. I kept this piece of infor-mation to myself, as there was nobody in those days who could re-wire us, and anyway we couldn't afford to have it done. Later on, and I will tell you about it in due course, we did go up in smoke, but that had nothing to do with the cable.

Nicky, the garage owner, was a dabster with plaster. He was a very nattily attired gent and while Chloe oo-hed and ah-ed, he would remove his coat, revealing a perfectly laundered shirt and gold cuff links, and get the job done in ten minutes, bless him!

When the middle room was properly illumined, my immediate re-action was to switch off the light at once. Never have I encountered such confusion. Stone pots of jam were holding down old boys' photographs, invoices, receipts, statements and catalogues were strewn over the floor, all coated with a conglomerate mixture of sugar, flour, and margarine. There were cups with broken handles, teapots without spouts, empty cake tins, saucepans, cooking pots, letters, scarves, gloves, magazines, all shoved into corners or spilling from a huge desk. Above all, the reserves of sugar, margarine and flour which I fondly imagined Chloe kept in the fastnesses of the larder, were dumped around the room itself. One large sack sat on the stairs, making them almost impossible to navigate, and the others were plumped behind the basket chair and in the fireplace. It must be admitted that the actual reserves were carefully closed, but the carrying of replenishments to the kitchen inevitably resulted in spillage and ullage.

It took ages to clear the place, during which time we discreetly turned off the light during opening hours. The 'vanguard' shifted the flour, sugar and marge to a place we had cleared in the kitchen so that neither of us need grope any longer. Chloe thoroughly approved of this plan, thank goodness. 'I never fort of vat,' she remarked.

But she didn't approve of my attempted elimination of the resultant spiders – Eric's progeny no doubt. As I've said, I had to wait until she wasn't looking to remove the great hairy things.

'If you wish to live and thrive,
Let a spider run alive,'

she chanted, always insisting that the largest and hairiest was Eric himself. I had no objection to them running alive, so long as they didn't do it in our middle room.

I also saw signs of mice (lucky mice) which I didn't like. Chloe's white cat 'Cupid' had 'joined up, dear,' several years ago during Chloe's last bout of bronchitis. Some recruits had taken him off in a jeep as a mascot. Poor Cupid! I often wonder what became of him, though he was a raw-boned unlovable beast, and his white fur showed everywhere when he was moulting. When Chloe in person saw two mice playing 'thee-thaw' on the scales, we both felt it was time to introduce Claudie.

Claudie was a perfect tea-room cat. He was grey-blue with amber eyes, not a thoroughbred – for he had a black brother in Windsor – but his manners, except for one or two notable lapses, were impeccable. He would ignore cat-haters, but mince up to cat-worshippers, saying in obvious cat-language that they were the one and only person he wished to meet. We never taught him, but he could beg just like a dog, waving his silvery paws in the air, and when invited, he would jump and settle on a welcoming lap, thus ensuring that his victim stayed another half-hour or so in order not to disturb him. This usually resulted in their ordering another pot of tea, or what-have-you, thus helping along the profits. He was such a good mouser too that it seems ungrateful to dwell on the fact that he was a little apt to leave the hind-parts of his catch in the path of his favourite customer. Likewise, he had a propensity for chocolate cake which I have never encountered again in any cat; but they are all individualists and he never stole anything else.

'I wish we could have a cart-horse as a pet,' sighed Chloe after one of Claudie's minor misdemeanours. (I had a momentary vision of an immense cart-horse hob-nobbing with the Dames in our cramped middle room.) 'This place isn't big enough tho',' she ruminated regretfully. 'And I don't suppose they can catch mice.'

I assented with relief.

'It seems a pity,' she continued to mourn. 'They have such lovely feet.'

There, mercifully, the matter rested.

But to return briefly to that horrible middle room; after days of effort during which the enormous desk was precariously hoisted over High Street into the first-floor window of Chloe's sitting-room and replaced by a painstakingly stained kitchen dresser, on which were arranged the blue and white teacups and saucers, the plates, cutlery, and jams, I dramatically turned up the light to show off my handiwork to Chloe.

'It looks awfully bare and unhomely,' she commented. 'And you can see now that Mr Churchill has gone mouldy.'

She referred to a large, currently popular, poster of Mr Churchill pointing out something or other which she had cunningly pasted over a damp patch on the wall near the cake table. Kelly did not approve of her doing it. 'Never reveal your political affiliations in business,' he advised.

I suppose that was good advice really, but as most of our customers couldn't have been truer or bluer (and anyway you couldn't see Churchill very well) we didn't take advantage of it. We merely hung a net curtain over my carefully polished window and inserted a dimmer bulb.

* * * * *

'Ex-thra-ordinary fing, dear,' said Chloe approvingly as I helped her rearrange the cakes before the rush of boys, 'you seem to have been here munfs and munfs.'

Certainly it was true that after a few weeks of her easy-going regime, my character, shrivelled by years of taking orders, seemed to expand and blossom. No longer did I cower in the background but took my place serving and chatting up the customers.

'The washing-up doesn't get done so quickly,' I grinned.

Soon I also discovered an attribute I didn't know I possessed. It can only be called Latent Ferocity. I think it must be the same quality that school teachers develop for quelling unruly pupils, but I never had need of it before. I suppose the Nasty Jam Man ought to be thanked for revealing it, for it has since occasionally stood me in very good stead.

'Why ever do you order so much jam?' I asked Chloe one day.

'I don't, dear,' she replied. 'It's that dreadful Jam Man. I'm never up when he gets here, and he sends me just what he finks he will.'

The tea customers were given generous helpings, though only a limited amount of jam could be used in cooking cakes. However, the murky middle room was absolutely studded with pots of jam.

'Well, couldn't we order it by post?' I asked Chloe.

'Oh *no*!' returned Chloe, scandalised. 'The poor man would lose his commission.'

Chloe at that time knew much more about travellers and representatives than I did, though she rarely seemed to encounter them face to face. Until that date in my life I had only had to deal with the gentlemanly patent medicine brigade on the doctors' doorsteps. Apparently, before the war, Chloe had been allowed to decant this firm's excellent jams and preserves into smaller jars, label them inexpertly and sell them to unsuspecting customers, who thought they were home-made. Now that jam was strictly rationed, we weren't allowed to do this, but it explained the comparatively large allocation we were given. What the Nasty Jam Man had given Chloe to understand was that unless she took up the whole allocation every time, she would be deprived of all our jam. This may have been a genuine misunderstanding on her part, but I too took an instant dislike to this person when we ultimately met.

He must have been delayed somewhere because Chloe and I were together when he majestically strode in like a rajah and selected our most comfortable tea-room chair.

'Ah! I've just time for a cuppa,' he boomed without even being asked if he'd like one. He then launched into a rather questionable anecdote, and looked intently at us with his pig-like eyes to see how we took it. Chloe managed a rather sickly smile, but something at the nape of my neck began to prickle in the same way I suppose as Claudie's tail bushed when he encountered a foe.

'Now,' cried the Nasty Jam Man beginning to fill in the delivery order, 'the usual, I suppose?'

'We want one pot of apricot jam only,' I ordered.

'*What!*' roared the Jam Man. 'What about the other fifty pounds you are entitled to?'

'WE DON'T REQUIRE THEM THIS MONTH!' I shouted, my

voice rising screechily. I could feel myself sweating and going puce in the face. 'We are overstocked for the present.'

'You will let us have some more when we want it, won't you?' Chloe chipped in quaveringly.

'Of course he will,' I snapped at her. 'We have an allocation, haven't we?'

A good deal of bounce had evaporated from the Nasty Jam Man by this time, but when Chloe departed like a chidden cur into the kitchen, I gave the poor man the full works, waxing eloquent on the viciousness of deceiving invalidish and unsuspecting old ladies.

'Well,' he faltered as he gulped down his scalding coffee, 'seven pounds of apricot this time, and to ask you again before I order more?'

'Correct!' I roared ferociously as he plunged into the street.

'Really, I was scared to deff of you!' gasped Chloe as I joined her in the kitchen and apologised for being so discourteous.

I never launched my newly-found furious behaviour on the boys: there wasn't any need. But now and then I found it quite useful. Once for instance an unmistakable aroma of alcohol invaded the middle room, accompanied by raucous laughter coming from the tea-room. One of Claudie's admirers who had been sitting there too, crept in to us and whispered that four 'gentlemen' were lacing their coffee with the contents of a bottle of rum they had brought with them.

'I wonder where they got it from?' was Chloe's first reaction. She loved a tipple: but as the 'gentlemen' became noisier, she decided that 'dear ole Peg should do somefing'.

'Dear ole Peg' began to swell visibly. Without thinking about it too much, she strode in on them . . . Did they think our exclusive establishment was a common pub? Did they not know that the shop would be banned to half our Eton clientele if it were found that alcohol was being consumed on the premises? Did they not know that 'gentlemen' removed their headgear in this kind of place? They sheepishly removed their hats, then almost immediately replaced them and slunk out, leaving me a tip I didn't deserve! Anybody who has not experienced this sort of thing can imagine the satisfaction it gives to the habitually mild-mannered.

By no means all the travellers were like the Nasty Jam Man. In fact they were as varied and interesting as any other crowd of men, and they certainly didn't, like sailors, maintain a 'wife in every port' as I had fondly imagined. For the most part we became genuinely involved in concern about their children's tonsils or their dying old mothers, and when they left or retired, we felt for a time really forlorn without them.

When I first joined Chloe, the grocery representative seemed to be managed by a kind of remote control. He was a dear old man with a white walrus moustache, and went to a great deal of trouble to try and divine what 'the lady' was likely to want. (Incidentally nobody could pronounce the name Chloe. Some called us Messrs. Choles, others merely 112 High Street, and the milkman called us Red Step because of the red ochre we used outside.) Dear old Mr Clark seemed really to worry about us, and I think it was a relief to him when, after suitable initiation, I took on the ordering. At first he would murmur at me: 'She had the flour last week and she's not yet entitled to her sugar ration . . . I wonder if she'd like dates until the dried fruit comes in. It isn't in yet . . . or she might like prunes. Cut up they can be quite tasty in a cake.'

I soon got to know his day for calling and made efforts to find out what we really did want, for even Mr Clark could make errors of judgment, such as the time he sent us two dozen jars of piccalilli pickles merely because they were in short supply. After the business of ordering was over, he would strain his coffee through his moustache with gusto, and treat me to a résumé of Sunday's sermon. He and half his family by all accounts sang in the choir of their little suburban church. He never left without thanking us for 'That nice refresher', and it was a sad day for us when he was finally superannuated.

Young Mr Knowles was another favourite. He had something important wrong with his insides and could not therefore be called up. I can't remember what he travelled in – possibly it was dried egg. The Ministry of Food just allocated traders for this nasty stuff and we had no choice where to go. At any rate we were lucky in being given Mr Knowles. He was an under-sized, gentle little man, who had to be revived with our most succulent wares and who aroused our maternal instincts. Once he arrived panting and apologetic just after closing hours. He had been sitting by the roadside with a badly hurt ownerless dog which had been run over. The driver of the car who had done the deed had at least telephoned for a vet, but our kind Mr Knowles wouldn't let it suffer alone and stayed beside it until the vet came and put it out of its misery.

4
Benevolent Aunties

With a few notable exceptions I came to love our travellers and looked forward to their visits. But on all counts the boys inspired our affections the most. They were young, carefree and had enormous appetites. The only fly in the ointment as far as we were concerned was that for four long months of the year they were away. Perhaps if holidays had been shorter, the teashop would have become the gold mine everyone predicted. On the other hand these breaks did give us a chance to recoup our energies, and sometimes when business previously had been good, we ourselves shut up shop and relaxed for a few days.

I think the boys must have regarded us as slightly feeble-minded though benevolent aunties. Certainly we never had any Trouble (with a capital T) with them. Even Kelly and Shaw at the chemist's had to display easily pocketable goods under glass, and the stamp shop man was reputed to have bodily thrown out a youngster he caught trying to pinch a stamp. Somebody discussing this phenomenon with me pronounced rather pompously: 'Chloe treats them all like gentlemen and so they behave like them.'

There may have been something in that, I suppose, but the fact remains that they mostly totted up their own bills correctly, and although they often invaded the kitchen to see what crumbs of icing sugar or sultanas were about, I never saw anyone take a cake and not pay for it. Naturally they weren't paragons of virtue. Once when I wasn't around they locked Chloe in the larder, and went off. But they returned pretty soon to see if she was all right. A rather more traumatic occasion was when we allowed a couple of boys to ice one of our cakes themselves. It looked rather horrible when they had finished, but they seemed inordinately proud as they raced off with it to be in time for boys' dinner. Almost immediately Kelly dashed across the road in his white coat. This in itself was a danger sign, as like Chloe, he always spruced up before emerging on to the public highway.

'Er – did those last two boys make any purr-chases to take away?' he asked breathlessly.

'Yes,' replied Chloe unsuspectingly. 'They iced one of our cakes with chocolate icing. It looked awful, but they seemed to be pleased with it.'

Kelly eyed us darkly. 'Aye!' he said meaningfully. 'It would be chocolate all right. D'ye know them?'

'They aren't regulars, and we don't know their names, if that's what you mean,' Chloe replied. 'But what's wrong?'

A lot of explanation followed, from which it transpired that the boys had come chattering and laughing into Kelly's shop and bought an unusual amount of a medicinal chocolate used to combat constipation. It was rather expensive, and Kelly vaguely wondered as he watched them cross the road to us why they bought so much. By the time he had realised what might be happening, it was too late.

'They'll probably offer pieces to their wurrst enemies,' Kelly suggested.

'They won't die, or anyfing will they?' Chloe asked in some agitation, though her eyes were dancing.

'Oh, no-o-o,' Kelly soothed. 'But they could be verry uncomfortable for a day or two.'

We were rather anxious for a time, for indubitably it was one of our cakes, though by the time the boys had finished with it it wasn't really recognisable. All the same, Mrs 'Sea-Shell Inn' down the road had recently been put out of bounds for some unspecified offence, and as far as we knew we might be the next to be so treated. Kelly, always a sound adviser, counselled complete silence about the whole affair. We found this difficult, but concurred with his good sense. There was nothing much we could do about it anyway, apart from alerting the whole school. After a few weeks, when danger of being found out receded, I hit on a plan to discover what the consequences, if any, had been. I paid a social call on my successor, Betty, at the doctors' bearing with me some new trifle from the shop for her to sample as an excuse for calling. After the usual pleasantries, I asked if she had been busy.

'Not very,' she replied. (She was far more efficient than I: I was always busy there.)

'No epidemics?' I asked diplomatically.

Betty jumped to the bait. 'No', she said, 'not really, one house,' (and she named it) 'had a series of stomach upsets last week, including the Dame. The cause wasn't traced, but it hasn't spread and they seem to have got better. It must have been some bug, I suppose.'

My question was answered! Much later I asked a trusty boy whom I had come to know well, and who boarded in the self-same house, actually what *had* happened.

'Oh!' he said, casually. 'Most of us knew about it. The fellas gave the whole cake to m'Dame, who ate several pieces and was awfully ill, and the rest went to her nasty little favourites who sucked up to her and got invited to tea.'

Such is the loyalty of boys to their fellows that none of this had leaked out – which was perhaps fortunate for us!

Another potentially tricky episode occurred one day when, coming back from lunch, Chloe stopped me flinging my outdoor things on the stairs – my usual custom.

'I'm lettin' two boys change in the barf-room,' she said, 'and they might fall over your coat.'

'Whatever do they want to do that for?' I enquired.

'Don't know really,' she replied vaguely. 'They said they couldn't get back to the house in time, or somefing.'

Soon we heard them stumping downstairs. At the sight of them Chloe and I were stupefied. They appeared to be almost as broad as they were long. Three overcoats at least covered them, the largest and longest reaching to the bottom of their regulation striped trousers which were tucked into the tops of black football boots. Round their necks and chins were coiled huge woolly scarves, and the whole ensemble was topped by two unlikely-looking cloth caps. They looked for all the world like Strube's little men facing a snowstorm. Valiant Claudie fled for his life.

Chloe recovered herself first. 'Won't you be rarver hot?' she asked. 'It's quite warm out.'

'Oh no!' came a muffled voice within the coils. 'My friend and I feel the cold.'

'Well, remember we shut at six o'clock,' Chloe adjured.

'Oh, we'll be back for absence,' (roll call) came the muted reply.

'Whatever are they up to?' Chloe gasped. 'They look like burglars...'

Back they came, with about five minutes to spare. Puce in the face, they rushed upstairs, bundled out of their clothes and reappeared looking more or less their former selves in the space of one minute flat.

'We'll collect our things tomorrow,' they panted as they rushed away.

Nicky was our first customer the next morning. He always was a cheery person, but today he was even more bouncy.

'You seem very pleased with yourself today,' Chloe lisped.

'And why not?' returned Nicky. 'I'm not a racing man, but yesterday I went with a friend, just for the hell of it, and won twenty pounds.'

'Good gracious!' we said simultaneously. 'Was it the Windsor Races yesterday?'

'Yes, of course it was,' he replied. 'The last day!'

Light dawned on us immediately. That was where those young ruffians had been going. We must have exchanged meaning looks.

'What's the matter?' asked Nicky, sensing our discomposure.

'Oh! Nuffin really!' replied Chloe hastily, and launched into a well-worn story of how her pore ole farver had won the Goodwood Stakes in 1881 with Brown Bess, while I sloped off to get his order.

When the culprits returned to collect their gear, we were quite nice to them, but by common consent vetoed their ever using our premises again for such a purpose.

'You see,' Chloe explained, 'it's our livelihood, and if anyone caught you emergin' from here in those awful clo's, boys might be forbidden comin' here at all.'

They were eminently reasonable and promised not to embarrass us again in such a way. Indeed, one of them later became quite a good legitimate customer.

It was inevitable that we should have our favourites. Mostly mine were the lost-looking waif-like misfits who looked as if their 'mother's milk were scarce out' of them. Chloe characteristically preferred the handsome ones, especially members of Pop. Boys in Pop, to inform the uninitiated, were the cream of the College. It consisted of twenty-four boys elected among themselves, and comprised Captain of Boats, Captain of the XI, Captain of the Oppidans, Captain of the School, some, but not all, House Captains, and outstanding personalities throughout the School. Their official title was 'Eton Society' and, unlike the Dames, they had their own common room and special fags to run hither and thither for them. Moreover, they were privileged at all times to carry a furled umbrella, wear a flower in the buttonhole of their braided tail-coat, spongebag trousers, and a coloured waistcoat. Their top-hats could have 'Pop' stamped in sealing wax on the brim, but we noticed that the most fastidious had their seals stamped inside the high crown. Naturally, even in wartime they took enormous care over their appearance, and Chloe was entranced. When only one or two of them were left in the shop she would even exclaim admiringly: 'Oh! What gorgeous waistcoats!'

If a Beak, a Dame, or another boy, had said such a thing to these lofty youths, the remark would have been disdainfully ignored; but Chloe seemed to get away with it. Her spontaneous homage seemed to melt them: they preened.

'I must show you my best one,' one would say.

'Mine is made of curtain material,' said another, displaying his majestically brocaded bosom. Clothes rationing was then extremely strict, and Chloe of course would compliment him on his ingenuity.

At another time a particular favourite told her he had managed to obtain some plain ivory satin from his grandmother, and he was getting 'Mrs Bunny Shop' – the babywear establishment up the street – to embroider pink rosebuds all over it. He would then ask Walls, the tailors, to manufacture him a superb waistcoat, though I don't remember that we ever saw that one.

It is difficult to convey in words the awesome magnificence of these chaps, and I am fully aware of the scorn that the pro-comprehensive brotherhood will pour on me; but let me stick to my opinions and let them abide by theirs!

Before I became a teashop lady I was introduced to the mother of a boy in Pop – an Australian. 'I suppose you have been stuck over here since the War broke out?' I condoled.

'Most certainly not,' she replied. 'I landed last week. My husband had to pull a few strings, of course.'

I expressed surprise that she had braved such a journey.

'W-a-a-l,' she drawled with an endearing smile, 'my English friends down under told me my boy – Captain of the Cricket XI at Eton and in Pop – would never in the whole of his life be so splendid or important as he is now, and I felt I must be in on it!'

So this intrepid woman had braved the long sea-journey from Australia with the ever imminent risk of being blown out of the sea by depth charges or attacked from above by bombers, just to share in her son's glory. Chloe, in similar circumstances, and had she had the money, would have done exactly the same.

When we first joined forces, Chloe was bewailing the loss of two of her favourites. 'It seems as soon as you get to know them, they have to leave,' she lisped.

The first one was Guy Plunkett – a boy I never saw, but who was undoubtedly a great ally and help to her. Chloe thought he must have had 'somefing' wrong with his heart, for he was excused all games, and during the three half-holidays a week which Eton enjoyed, he could always be found helping her in the kitchen. His friends called him 'Chloe's partner'. He expected to become an eminent doctor after he left, and during succeeding years she often referred to him and wondered what had become of him. But she never heard. Perhaps the 'somefing' caught up with him.

I think the other one, Tennant, and I, overlapped by about one half (term). He was a handsome, engaging youth whose mother held the possibly mistaken, or at least exaggerated, view that Chloe had a Good Influence on him. Be that as it may, the whole family were delightful to us, even inviting us after the war to a pre-firework picnic on the Fourth of June. We couldn't accept of course, as the Fourth was the day when we hoped to recoup our wavering profits. When Tennant finally brought his 'leaving photograph' Chloe was near to tears, and a special shagreen frame in which to display it had to be selected from the chaos upstairs. Tennant's brother was still at the school, so we saw quite a bit of them before they too finally faded away.

We never knew the names of half the boys who came to us, and this in any case is not intended to be a name-dropping chronicle. 'Mrs Cock-pit', the famous luncheon and dinner place a little further up the street was the one for that. According to the irrepressible, but not always accurate boys, she kept two visitors' books, one for people with titles and one for mere customers. Inevitably this led to Brown mi. booking a table there for lunch for his parents under the name, say, of Lieutenant Colonel The Lord Brown, to be assured of a place.

We, ourselves, tended to overlook or forget the boring boys – the ones who already looked like their prosperous fathers – and take to our hearts the interesting, the eccentric, the pathetic or the plainly funny ones.

Jeremy Thorpe (or 'Forpe' as Chloe called him) was one of these last. When his regulation top-hat wore out, he commandeered one belonging to his father, inches higher than the usual type, waisted, and with a curly brim. This he tended to wear sideways on his head, giving him the air of a youthful Champagne Charlie. I once heard him maintain on the radio programme *Any Questions* that he was a repugnant schoolboy. This simply is not true: he was an interesting talker even then, if one could catch him in serious vein, with interests reaching far beyond who would get his House Colours.

Simon Goldblatt, sometime Captain of the School, was another of our regulars, a madly clever boy, whose father was something very high in the Liberal hierarchy. However, on more than one occasion they ignored 'mouldy' Mr Churchill and helped us wash up. For one Fourth of June I tried very hard to force one of those enormous sunflowers for Simon to wear in his buttonhole. Unfortunately I couldn't do it, so he had to make do with an immense dahlia.

Then there was dear Varlien, about whom an entire book could be written. He first crossed our threshold as a diminutive little boy, clad in a bum-freezer and wearing so large a hat that it seemed only his rather large ears and nose kept him from being totally extinguished by it. Claudie took to him at once, and until he got bigger poor Varlien would sit uncomfortably in a dark corner, his toes just touching the ground so that this selfish beast should have as horizontal a lap as possible. He never breathed a word, but Chloe suspected that he originally came to us (usually in the afternoons) to get a bit of peace from unmerciful 'mobbing', an Eton word for ragging.

How right she was! A year or two later when he had lengthened, broadened and even grown into his topper, he took it into his head to repay in kind some of the indignities he had been subjected to when he was so small. With infinite deliberation he arranged a water jug over the door of every boy's study on his corridor, so that before they were able to get inside their rooms icy water would mercilessly sloosh down their necks. What he failed to do was to set one up over his own room door, so it didn't take long for his outraged victims to divine who had played them this trick. Retribution by six boys came sharply and swiftly. Varlien's boys' maid (who told us the story) arrived in time to find Varlien surveying the damage and contemplating revenge. Bedding, clothes, pictures, books, drawers and their contents were flung into a heap in the middle of the room. His window box was overturned on to that, and the whole mass liberally watered.

41

'Don't you do nothing, sir,' she advised. 'We'll get this to rights easy!'

So she and he set to work (in her own off-time) and in an hour everything was more or less orderly. Boys' maids were the salt of the earth in those days, and she had quite probably dealt with similar incidents before.

'Now, sir, when you hear them coming in, just swagger out dressed in your best, but don't say nothing,' she suggested.

Varlien did exactly that and (probably) came down and had a cup of tea with Chloe and me, though we heard nothing at all of this episode from him. The avenging boys were utterly dumbfounded. Had the House-beak or Dame seen the chaos? Had they been reported to someone? They lay low until the storm blew over and only Varlien and the boys' maid ever knew the full facts. I'm not sure if this anecdote has a moral, except that it is not the first time nor the last that faithful boys' maids helped to quell a near-riot.

In later years Varlien became a top-class flower arranger, a much sought-after commentator at point-to-point meetings, and a successful lawyer all at the same time. I was at his wedding, and he is now the proud father of four bouncing children.

When Chloe was on her own and before I joined her, the late Lord Tweedsmuir (John Buchan) used to bring his boys in to tea.

'They had wonderful manners, dear,' Chloe told me. 'They used to stand up every time I went to see if they had everyfin'– quite unnervin', especially as I forgot everyfin' and had to go back lots of times. I got quite cross with them bobbin' up and down, and in the end said to them: "Oh for goodness sake keep still!" They did what I asked, but I don't fink their farver liked it.'

So many faces slip through my mind as well as a few names that it is impossible to tell about them all, and I am sure I will have left out some of our dearest. There was a Hambro – though I don't know which one – there were lots in the school. Our Hambro looked as if he were full of doughnuts! There was Teddy Millington-Drake – a gentle melting boy, also much beloved by our cat, and rather over-shadowed by the exploits of a brilliant father. Brian Berridge was another boy of whom we were particularly fond. He was a mature, thinking person, sometime Captain of Shooting. When he finally left he specially brought his mother to say goodbye and to thank us. Later he brought his tiny fiancée to see us and be approved of.

The greatest number of Chloe's cakes eaten at one sitting – fifteen in all – was devoured by a huge person destined to join the Grenadier Guards at Windsor. We had a serious conversation once as to how he and his bearskin would fit into the shop; but I don't think it was ever put to the test.

One of the few advantages enjoyed by Chloe and me was that the teashop was situated on the west side of High Street, which was the side on which Etonians were obliged to walk. The College had a great many ancient and weird rules, such as no boy being allowed to possess a wife, a beard or a badger, but whether this one was a rule or a mere convention, we didn't know. At any rate, I think it stood us in good stead. Boys were allowed to cross to shops opposite, but never to promenade along the other side. Hills and Saunders, the photographers, lay on the west side as well a little further up the street, and probably because of this Chloe and I were sometimes called on to pronounce verdicts on photographic proofs.

Now that everything is so expensive and the boys so (comparatively) poor, I don't know if the custom still persists, but throughout the time we were there boys leaving would order up to three dozen photographs which they would ceremoniously present to their tutors, Dames, friends and various allies on their last day at school.

'Isn't it a pity that only the most hideous boys seem to want our opinion,' Chloe would sigh. Indeed it did seem like that, but there must have been some good-looking proofs too, I suppose. We possessed quite a number of leaving photos ourselves, but not nearly as many as the Dames, some of whom had screens made entirely of them. Except for the sanctified Colin Tennant in his shagreen frame, we managed to confine ours to those long, glass-covered contraptions which held several photographs at a time, the shape of which helped to mask the damp patches on the middle room walls. Whoever the boy, we always privately mourned his departure and entry into adult life. They were always so different when they came back to see us.

*   *   *   *   *

The war went on inexorably. Eton had its bombs, and part of the nice old Georgian bit, Upper School, was wrecked, as well as the home of popular old 'Daddy Ley' the organist. Both Dr and Mrs Ley were in the house at the time and were looking at a cartoon in *Punch* which Mrs Ley maintained was just like her husband. He had just crossed the room to look over her shoulder when the bomb fell, and the armchair in which he had been sitting a few seconds before was flattened.

Nothing was left of their home. Of course, everyone rallied round as they always do in an emergency, but they were a childless couple and their lost pets caused them much heart-ache. Happily, after two days, Pussy emerged from the ruins, and two days after that their spaniel Simon turned up. Both animals were unrecognisably filthy and very thirsty, but were otherwise uninjured. I met Dr Ley in the street that day. He was grinning from ear to ear and Simon, newly shampooed, was in his arms. Their home and treasures were gone, but war was apt to invest people with a different set of values.

Miss Iredale Smith, Matron in College (the only so-called 'Matron' at Eton), told us that at this time she had a suspect measles case in the sick room adjoining Upper School. Undaunted, she courageously pounded through the choking brick dust, rubble and debris to rescue the lad. When she got there, he was cheerfully sitting up in bed, with a window frame round his neck and surrounded by cascades of broken glass, but without having sustained a scratch!

But I digress: to return to Chloe and me and the teashop, we scrambled along somehow in spite of, or sometimes I thought *because* of, the shortages. When one week we had no sugar, we substituted jam. When we had no dried fruit, we made shortbread. At one time our mixtures had to be 'scone-ified' – eked out with dates – as neither the margarine nor the sultanas had come. (Yeast cooking was not possible, it would have been poaching on the baker's preserves.) For, however short we ourselves were of materials for cooking, one could be sure that the unfortunate householder had less. It isn't easy to recall now how one pound pot of jam or marmalade had to last one person a month, and four ounces of sugar last a week. Curious contraptions for siphoning the cream off the top of the milk were very much in vogue so that it could be shaken into butter and added to our weekly two ounces, though milk too was rationed. And there was a fearsome wartime recipe for making three pounds of marmalade out of *one* orange, two ounces of sugar, carrots, and turmeric – that yellow material you get in pickles. It was as horrible as it sounds!

Paint peeled from our fascia, and our shop window got grimier and grimier, as there was nobody able-bodied enough, or with time to spare, to clean it. I made a mighty effort once and tried to rub up our black paint with shoe polish, but it wasn't very successful, and brought down imprecations on my head when at last we did manage to obtain paint and a painter.

5
The Margarine Miracle

Teashop-wise, peace when it eventually came was almost as grim as the war. Naturally we were relieved that idiotic people throughout the world had stopped killing each other. 'It all th-eems th-o th-illy!' Chloe would lisp repeatedly at the height of hostilities. But we didn't like the aftermath. Shortages became really acute, and horrid little coupons called 'Bread Units' (B.U.s for short) had to be cut out of customers' ration books for every eight ounces of cakes we sold. These had to be counted weekly and sent in to the Food Office. Paper was in very short supply so B.U.s were perforce very small. Once, in the middle of counting them, Chloe, who had a streaming cold, gave an unexpected sneeze, with the chaotic result that B.U.s flew in all directions – under the gas-stove, between the baking tins, in our hair, and everywhere you could think of. Aggravatingly, and with maximum maledictions we had to set to work re-counting them all over again.

As well as this, our meagre ration of margarine was cut down by so large a percentage that we expected after our current stocks were exhausted to have to close down.

Electricity too was rigidly rationed so that the cakes could no longer be displayed under the pink shade in the dark middle room. Chloe overcame this dilemma by rooting out from the miscellaneous jumble upstairs two tall, fat candles. Ordinary candles were unobtainable, and where in the dim-distant past she had picked up these from she couldn't remember. However, tucked into my mother's best candlesticks, they added an air of almost religious mystery to the cakes. The problem was whether they would outlast the electricity cuts. In actual fact they just did so, with about four inches to spare.

It was about this time that I had a Red Letter day. David Attlee, the doctor's son, was already a friend and ally. He had been at the school at the time I worked for his father, but meanwhile had joined

45

up and by the time I went to Chloe's he was recovering from a beastly thigh wound received at El Alamein. While still convalescing, he improved the shining hour by making us a cupboard which hid a multitude of debris; but what inspired him to invite me to London for the day I shall never know. I was nearly twenty years his senior, and surely it is unusual for a young-man-about-town, as he was then, to give treats to his father's rather dilapidated ex-secretary.

Chloe and I went into a huddle as to What-I-Should-Wear. She had managed to tidy me up a little for the teashop, but I could scarcely face the metropolis in a flowered overall. Eventually we mustered a neat, dark-blue coat (Chloe's), my sister's gloves and excruciatingly uncomfortable shoes, and a hat (unrationed) specially bought for the occasion, on which Chloe artistically arranged an eye veil. Viewed from this distance of time, I realise this outfit sounds excessively un-adventurous, but the mere fact of wearing something different, even a little soignée, did much for my morale.

We went first in a taxi to the Ritz for a drink – the one and only time I have been within its portals. It looked grand, dirty and expen-sive, but I'm glad I went there and saw the bell boys walking around with names written on slates to call people to the telephone. I suppose everything must be mechanical now – loud speakers and so on – not nearly so dignified and relaxing.

Having thus refreshed ourselves, David then took me for lunch to one of his haunts in Soho run exclusively by a family of Anglo-Italians, where he assured me the food tasted pre-war. It certainly was deliciously unusual, especially washed down with a bottle of Chianti. By the time the coffee came, we were both mellow and pleased with life. It was only then that it almost casually slipped out that Chloe and I would have to shut down because of our cut ration of margarine.

'*What!*' exclaimed David. 'You can't do that! What would happen to Chloe? *You* might get on all right, but what about her? She's much too old to get taken on anywhere.'

I admitted guiltily that we had rather been living in a fool's paradise while our present stocks lasted. But what could be done anyway?

'Come on,' he urged, as he hastily paid the bill and summoned another taxi. 'We're going to the House of Commons.'

I trembled. Even a quart of chianti would not have given me that much courage had I been alone, but David was adamant. Firmly, he marched me into a lofty, dingy, ante-cum-waiting room. This part of the House of Commons had not been bombed, but brick dust is all pervasive and, except for the pretty tiled floor, I was unimpressed. It only later dawned on my benighted intellect that this was the famous Lobby one reads about, and that I was *Lobbying my MP!*

We were approached by a personage of great dignity who asked our business.

'This lady wishes to have a word with her Member,' announced David portentiously.

'They are in debate at the moment,' replied this majestic official, 'but if you will write down your name, address, and subject for discussion, I will see that he is given the note.' He then swept off to other encounters.

'Who on earth *is* your MP?' hissed David, who had quite overlooked this detail.

Eton is attached to Slough, not Windsor, for voting purposes, but memories of discussions with Ed Kelly under the eye of the mouldy Churchill poster stood me in good stead. 'Mr Fenner Brockway,' I whispered. 'But what on earth shall we write?'

I ought to have explained before, that when the thigh wound abruptly ended David's army career, and after Oxford, he had got a job in London as a sub-editor on the *Daily Mail*, so that he had the ready word.

'Put something like "Old lady of seventy-five unable to make a living because of the recent reduction in margarine ration," ' he suggested. 'And I'll sign it too for good measure. The name might help.' (David was in fact distantly related to Prime Minister Attlee, though they had scarcely met.)

In less than ten minutes Mr Fenner Brockway emerged from a little side door – presumably The Chamber. There was no television in those days, and I think I expected him to be ten feet high or hung with chains of office or something. Actually his appearance was less impressive than the flunkey at the door.

'Let's go and have a cup of tea,' were his first words.

Replete to overflowing with spaghetti Bolognese, cheese, chianti and coffee, this was the last thing that either of us wanted, but we both divined that it was what my Member craved, and possibly what had brought him out so quickly. Indeed, it might have been that the poor man had missed lunch altogether.

'Thank you very much, sir,' smiled David, limping with us to the lift and looking exactly like the best brand of wounded British soldier – which of course he was! I too murmured my delight.

The canteen to which we went was a great disappointment! I must have read in novels about dining on the terraces, I suppose, and this small room, with a counter at one end displaying a few unappetising buns, bare tables and hard wooden chairs, was a dismal revelation. Except for a large electric bell fixed on the wall by the clock behind the assistant's head (which I rightly took to be the Division Bell), the whole place might have been mistaken for a rather seedy pull-up for car-men.

However, we got a huge brown pot of tea, and Mr Fenner Brockway, having downed half a large cupful in a gulp and beginning to munch one of the terrible buns, asked what was our trouble.

I had got it off pat by now, and explained fairly lucidly, I think, that if our margarine ration were reduced by this huge percentage, Chloe and I would be out of business. Mr Fenner Brockway's first question was to ask if there was any other business in our town similarly placed. Possibly he thought we were trying to pull a fast one on a rival. On being assured that we were the only home-made cakeshop for miles, he fixed his eyes on David and in so many words asked why he was with me.

'I haven't any right to be here at all,' answered David disarmingly. 'Except I don't want to see my old friends give up a small but flourishing trade.'

'Are you related to the PM?' he asked, his mouth full of bun.

'Not very closely, sir. My father and he are first cousins, I think.'

Tea appeared to mellow our Member. He listened attentively (a very unusual phenomenon in MPs generally, I believe), and after he had eaten his third excruciating bun and drunk the tea-pot dry, he had sympathetically promised to speak to the Minister of Food about it. We said goodbye with great cordiality, and although nothing really had altered at that stage, both David and I felt we had an ally in high places.

We hadn't much time left after that, for I had to get back for tomorrow's baking, and David had to get some sleep before his nightly sub-editing stint. So of all places we went to the Zoo. Some would say this was from the sublime to the ridiculous – or the other way round – but David had a yen for the African elephant, and I had never seen the giant panda, the late lamented Chi Chi.

It came to an end much too soon, but the very next day (posts worked better than they do now), I received a letter from Charles Hill, Minister of Food, telling me that the Cooking Fats Order would be amended so that all small traders working on the present minimum ration would not have their present allocations cut...I wish Chloe had been around when *both* our margarine men were later promoted to the House of Lords – bless them!

*　　*　　*　　*　　*

This was the era when Eton began subtly to change. Men home from the forces began trickling back into civilian jobs. From our point of view this meant the gradual disappearance of elderly Beaks who during the war had been dug out of retirement to allow the younger masters to enlist. On the whole they had been a silent crowd who came for a quick coffee and a quick warm up before charging off to take other classes. Until they were required to leave Eton, they hardly impinged on our consciousness at all and we scarcely exchanged two words with them, but under notice they seemed to become garrulous. They were mostly widowers or bachelors, and Chloe formed the opinion that they were probably 'Goin' back to na-thty old houthkeepers'.

By and large we collected an amazing variety of customers. I suppose the smallness and intimacy of the place attracted them. Once I was astonished to find the tea-room crammed with the blackest of black negresses, their dazzling smiles flashing in their polished faces, and their bright turbans contrasting with our flowers. I suppose they were having a conducted tour of the College.

'You'll get a shock when you go in there,' I warned Chloe, as I came out with an order for fifteen coffees.

'Don't they match the tables!' exclaimed Chloe, in a hoarse whisper which I hope they didn't hear.

Another time there was the lugubrious lemon-coloured little man who came and reserved a table for tea for a week for five small children with whom he was shooting a short film down the road. Five small children on their own let loose among our cakes caused me some misgivings, which I voiced.

'Oh, it's all right,' he drawled in a Canadian-cum-Cockney accent. 'They'll come with their chaperon. I want the kids to get a change of scene from the set, and some exercise. The principals are being looked after on site.'

Chaperon! What an out-of-context word! We didn't know what

49

to expect, but when she did turn up with her troupe, you couldn't distinguish her from one of the most senior (and severest) of old-fashioned Eton nannies. Under her hawk-like eye, the children behaved like cherubs.

'Scones and butter first,' she snapped. 'James, you eat too quickly ... Now you may have jam ... *James!* Little gentlemen *always* hand plates to ladies before taking their own helpings...' and so on, and so on.

'What extraordinarily well-behaved children!' I remarked, when the lemon-coloured man came to settle up.

'They have to be,' he responded grimly. 'Otherwise you'd have them running all over the set and getting in the way.'

'Where did you get your chaperon from?' I asked inquisitively.

'Oh she's an old trouper. Glad to do it,' he replied.

We were pleased to hear much later that the film, *A Stranger Comes to Town*, had won some sort of award – the best short of the year, I think. And well our little yellow man deserved it, because as we got to know him better, he divulged that he was suffering from 'the yellow jaundice' (is there another coloured variety?) and we tried to revive him on a diet of Bovril and dry bread.

Then there were the 'Afternooners' who were really rather a bore, except that we were sorry for them. We had not got to the stage when Chloe rested after lunch while I baked my share of cakes and served the odd tea. It soon became increasingly difficult for her to get away to lie down, so I unashamedly invented stern doctor's orders insisting that she should rest immediately after food. Essentially this was near enough to the truth, for what lady in her late seventies (as Chloe then was) should not rest in the afternoon, especially if later on she insisted on baking until the small hours? The only slight prevarication was the mention of a doctor, but it seemed to add weight to my statement. In fact it was well-nigh impossible to get her to see a doctor, unless she was confined to bed.

'They always give me the feelin' I'm goin' to die,' she asserted, 'like clergymen.'

Meanwhile, I was left with the pitiful 'Afternooners', or as Chloe called them, 'Peg's ole fings'. They were a varied collection whose names either I never knew, or have forgotten, but the one thing they had in common was their overwhelming desire for a sympathetic pair of ears to listen to them.

They would usually order coffee, and when it was brewed and

brought to them, they would do all in their power to keep one from going back to the kitchen. After several batches of over-cooked scones, I used to bow to the inevitable and invite them to sit in the middle room so that I could keep an eye on the cooking at the same time as hearing their woes. The nicest of them would ask if they could help – an offer never resisted in our establishment – and while embarking on what seemed to be total life-histories, they would rub in fat and flour for the rock buns, or swash about in the washing-up.

It needed a lot of concentration to keep the baking, the teas and the Afternooners going, but usually it was just possible. The stories I heard! I often felt myself a sort of secular Mother Confessor, and still cannot bring myself to record some of the revelations I heard.

Teashop ladies are supposed to know everything, I discovered. Could you be married in church without first being confirmed? Were there any ladies of easy virtue to be found in the neighbourhood (this last was from what Chloe would have called a very nath-ty man), and what are the first signs of VD? I could answer the first question with authority, but being as innocent as an unborn lamb on the other two, covered my ignorance with a hearty laugh, implying in effect, 'surely you don't need me to tell you that!'

Of the less confidential variety was the superannuated housekeeper whose 'lady', also superannuated, hung on to life by a thread. The housekeeper, who seemed to have every disease known to medical history, was also, it seemed to me, precariously balanced between earth and heaven. But she was determined to outlast her employer so that she would inherit the tidy little bequest she knew was coming to her. She was a nice old thing, and unselfish. She obviously deserved every penny of her inheritance, but she only really wanted it to help a beloved nephew establish the poultry farm he had just begun. She came Tuesday after Tuesday – her one free afternoon a week. Then silence, and no more visits. I still wonder which of the old ladies won!

Then there was a former cook at the Savoy, who, with his girl friend, had decided to abandon the West End and branch out 'where the money was', that was, Slough! He was Colonel Something-or-other, and they were apparently making money hand over fist in a sort of superior shack on the Slough Trading Estate. They came on their free afternoon to indulge in 'gracious living' again, at the expense of our roaring coal fire and my sponge buns. I didn't like them much, but I expect I was envious.

Dear old 'Mad Louise' was another matter. Our friendship lasted until her death about three years ago. When we first met she had a job in a bookshop in Windsor, and her fragile six-stone-odd was completely dominated by a huge black dog which tugged her unrelentingly where *he* wanted to go. Luckily for us both, 'Tigger' approved of the teashop in general and our cakes in particular, so during her rather late lunch breaks she was precipitated with much speed down Eton High Street by this rapacious hound to our place.

It isn't really very fair to call her 'Mad Louise', for in her eccentric way she was far from mad, but later we used the title to differentiate her from my grand-daughter, Louise, who always has her feet firmly on the ground.

Mad Louise had straight flaxen hair in those days, a beautiful complexion and sad, contemplative eyes. Claudie soon discovered that Tigger was no foe but acted as a delicious draught excluder in front of the fire.

'He's been brought up with cats all his life until now,' Louise explained when I first got to know her.

'I suppose you've got some at home?' I enquired.

'Not any more. They all had to go,' she replied, and looked about to cry.

'Oh dear!' was all I could find to say. 'I'd better get your coffee.'

When I got back, she had recovered her calm.

'Yes,' she said. 'They've all gone but Tigger – the goats, the geese, the chickens, and of course the cottage.'

'Oh dear!' I said again, knowing there was more to come. 'Come into the middle room with your coffee, and we can talk, if you like, while I do the cooking.'

Little by little and over the course of several visits it transpired that she had been married to a virile poet. Unfortunately for Louise (and for him too!), she had only 'fallen in love with his mind' and couldn't endure physical contact. So that part of the marriage was doomed to failure. After the death of her parents she spent most of the moderate capital they left her on buying a smallholding where she could indulge her obsessive love of animals, and he could have the peaceful atmosphere supposedly beloved by poets. Between them over the course of six or seven years they compiled and issued a free-thinking, way-out magazine, which nobody bought, but which cost Louise forty pounds a month to produce. I have never seen this publication, though I have read some of her husband's verses which were good. I fancy though that Louise's efforts were too airy-fairy for the general public's taste. Inevitably her capital dwindled, and there were debts. Louise, strictly brought up, became frantic. Husband, quite accustomed to living on tick and longing for the fleshpots, grew frantic for a local barmaid.

So Louise and he parted : the smallholding was sold and just covered the debts, and the marriage was ultimately annulled. The poet and the barmaid lived happily ever after, as far as I know, and raised a family, and as is the way of the world, poor penniless Louise was left with Tigger and a living to earn. She never complained, believing there were faults on both sides – which indeed there must have been.

After the marriage débâcle she never remained long in one place or one job, and my address book bulges with different addresses – Edinburgh, Bath, Bookham, Beaconsfield, Windsor, even Jamaica – to quote a few. At one time she was 'mad' enough to believe that she was able to augment the tail feathers of a pet parrot by sending healing rays through the post! But she was able to laugh at herself for her 'foolish notions' and enjoyed a little gentle teasing from us. She was likewise an enthusiastic exponent of Positive Thinking, which according to her rather vague interpretation was to be loving and affectionate to everyone. This precept overwhelmingly guided her to the day of her death. If more people were as 'mad' as she was, the world would be a good deal happier.

Toad was not an Afternooner in our sense of the word, though he visited us after lunch from time to time. Luckily he never remained long, as if a faithful Afternooner was already in situ, he would have been regarded with disapprobation. They liked the place and my ears to themselves. He was a mournful individual and the nickname fitted him, though it was by no means derogatory. He was one of the producers and leading lights of the Windsor Theatre and none other than Stanford Holme, husband of Thea, the author and book adapter. We called him Toad because just before we met we had seen his interpretation of Toad in A. A. Milne's *Toad of Toad Hall*, and had delighted in it.

'Oh! That's an easy part,' he lamented when we told him. I didn't believe him then and I don't now, for I have seen many other Toads since and none has matched his performance.

His connection with our teashop derived from his hobby of picking up Victorian jewellery. He liked mooching around Houndsditch market on a Sunday morning and buying anything that took his fancy. Victorian jewellery hadn't the vogue it enjoys today, nor was it so expensive: so we displayed in the window a dozen pieces or so in the small velvet-lined showcase he provided. I don't think either of us made a great deal of money out of it, but it provided an interest outside the theatre for him and it may have lured in tea customers for a closer look. I wish now I had bought some of his pieces. As well as the 'Mizpah's' and 'Dearest Mother's' with a curl of Victorian hair enclosed at the back, he sometimes brought delightful little crystal seals of doves, for instance, crying 'vite, vite' or tiny silhouette brooches of a coach and horses.

Chloe didn't really like any of the jewellery much. 'They're the sort of fings maids used to wear on their day out,' she lisped snobbishly.

Sometimes we were afflicted by a childish war-widow who ought to have engaged our sympathy, I suppose, but she started off on the wrong foot by asking if our beautiful witch ball which hung for decoration in the shop window indicated that we told fortunes.

'You see, I don't expect I'll ever get another boy with this,' she wailed, indicating her rather repulsive infant, gangling its arms and legs. 'So I just thought I'd ask.'

Chloe happened to be around that afternoon.

'What's its name?' I asked hastily, hoping to moderate Chloe's possible indignation.

'Thomasina, after her dad,' sighed the girl looking falsely pathetic. 'We only knew each other a month.'

I needn't have worried about Chloe's reaction. She was only listening with a quarter of her deaf old ears. 'Concertina!' she exclaimed, glancing at the wriggling infant. 'What an extraordinary name!'

*   *   *   *   *

Winifred Hope-Jones was never an 'Afternooner'. She had too much guts and courage. A great deal has been said and written about her husband, William, but nothing about his remarkable wife who was the pivot of the whole outfit. She was a large, smiling, chatty person, justly proud of her rumbustious family with whom she coped on very little money – by Eton standards at least. William was an affectionate but unavoidably remote person during his tenure of the House. She did the catering, got to know each boy individually, mothered the lonely ones and spurred on the ambitious. It was not easy for her when, at the beginning of the war, William, though by now of retiring age and able to give up the House, was asked to continue teaching while the younger masters joined the forces. Win took this all in her stride. Reduced from a domestic staff of eight to one faithful 'Nannie', she untiringly cooked, cleaned, sewed, repaired, and entertained all and sundry. She was the obvious person to fly to if you lost a button, failed to manage your sewing machine or merely wanted a bit of a chat and sympathy. Possessing no false personal pride, she acted as kitchen maid preparing vegetables in another boys' House when they were short-handed, and she quietly took on as well the repair of the choirboys' tattered surplices and cassocks which couldn't be renewed because of rationing. Another time she collected, washed, aired and returned the baby's nappies belonging to a slightly disorganised young mother. In fact she would hold out a helping hand to anyone unobtrusively and without fuss.

Inexorably as their age groups came up their sons went into the army. Then the cruellest thing that could happen to a parent took place. One of the three boys was posted missing. To keep up the spirits of the rest of this united family, Winifred positively affirmed that it was all an official muddle and that at any moment good old Kenneth would turn up demanding his favourite pudding. I don't think she managed to deceive the others, but she nearly convinced herself. Month after month went by, and in spite of many enquiries nothing was heard of him. Win saw to it that his bed was kept aired and his room cleaned and dusted regularly, and kept how he liked it. At length, over twelve months since he had first been posted missing, officialdom was able to inform William that their son had been killed on the very day they had first heard of his loss. From that moment the sparkle left Win. She continued to smile and carry out all the little kindnesses as before; sloshing meals at the British Restaurant (then installed in our church hall), handing on her meagre rations, giving house room to stranded people. Yet something had died in her, and from being the smooth-haired, plump, rosy-faced dancing-eyed woman of 1938, she became in a short time round-shouldered and haggard, with deep vertical wrinkles from cheek bones to jaw. She looked, in Chloe-parlance, 'mackintoshy', which denoted dull hair, dun-coloured clothes and skin and a general air of unkemptness. But there was nothing we could do to undermine her false cheerfulness and reserve, and as long as the family remained at Eton she was our loyal customer and friend.

Years later, after Winifred died, I married William. I was a ludicrous successor to Win, but I think she would have been glad to know there was someone around to look after him.

Grizel Hartley, wife of another House Master, was Chloe's top favourite, and they shared a common birthday (date, not year!) which seemed to emphasise her importance. In my memory she was a large junoesque individual of about fifty, with a sparkling smile for everyone, but those who remembered her coming to Eton as a bride said she had been ravishingly attractive – slim as a wand, with ripe corn-coloured hair, large blue-gray eyes, and a beautiful untouched-up complexion. The eyes and the complexion were still there, but there was more to Grizel Hartley than outward appearance.

She is a difficult person to describe, as her personality had so many facets. Large and liberal almost to a fault, one would have expected her to possess the open-handed, sprawling handwriting of the over-generous. Not a bit of it! She could squeeze more into a page of writing paper than an ordinary single-spaced typewriter could, and we lesser mortals had sometimes to use a magnifying glass to decipher it. She liked simple things, and the young Beak who gave her a present of tiny doll's notepaper earned full marks. On the other hand throughout the dreary old war when most people put their silver in the bank or even buried it in the garden, she insisted on every bit of hers being on show. Everyone invited to dine with her – be it merely wartime boiled cod and rhubarb – was expected to wear dinner jackets or long dresses. I think it was her way of cocking a snook at Hitler, but to those who went to her parties (mostly on bicycles in those days), it was an awful bore!

She had immense sympathy and understanding of the underdog, and her staff adored her and would do anything for her: so did Chloe – and with reason. Grizel would breeze into the middle room, an armful of garden flowers under one arm and a large shopping basket in the other.

'Miss Chloe is so fond of flowers!' she would say. 'Do give her these.'

Whatever Chloe was doing at the time, she would immediately drop it and fly to her like steel to a magnet, leaving me to carry on. They would retreat to the recesses of our awful kitchen, kiss, and Grizel would then probably give her some harmless piece of gossip, having the sense to speak very close to Chloe's ear, so that she could hear it. Chloe would be entranced, and sometimes, when nobody was looking, Grizel would dive into her capacious shopping basket and produce a bottle of whisky, 'To rid you of that cold, darling.' Everyone was 'darling' to Grizel.

The first time this happened, Chloe and I had a minor altercation about sharing the whisky. It now sounds a bit priggish of me but I refused to touch it, knowing full well what a lot of good it did her and how difficult it still was to obtain. She, on the other hand, adamantly refused to share it with anyone else or to drink alone.

'That's very bad luck,' she pronounced. Finally we compromised, and after much argument, we put a drop on the unfortunate Claudie's nose, and while he was disgustedly licking it off Chloe agreed to take a small tot herself.

Volumes could be written of the many intelligent kindnesses Grizel performed, not only to Chloe and me, but to everyone. She shared Chloe's gift, too, of making you feel much more attractive than you naturally are. Once she came into the shop just as I was emerging from putting a shilling in the meter. As I have explained previously, one had practically to stand on one's head to accomplish this feat, and my wiry red hair was literally standing on end.

'Darling!' exclaimed Grizel. 'You look like a chrysanthemum!'

6
The Fourth of June

I can't quite recall the circumstances that made Dicky our lodger. I
fancy Win must have had something to do with it. Chloe named her
Dicky almost at once, for she 'pecked' at her food like a 'little dicky
bird', but she was in fact Mabel Spurrier, an artist of great competence
but very little cash. She came down during summers hoping to obtain
orders from the boys for water-colour sketches of various parts of
Eton. These she executed meticulously and charged much too little
for. When it is too late for her to benefit from it, I feel sure the fashion
will revert to her faithful reproductions instead of the inaccurately
splashed on poster paint of today.

'All those windows!' she would expostulate in her soft little voice,
when faced with an order for a picture of a boy's House. Her client
could depend on each pane of glass and its highlight being represented
with his own study window well to the forefront. Instructions were
often given that his window-box should be made to look the most
luxurious. Dicky disliked doing boys' Houses, for they were mostly
ungainly Victorian monstrosities, but she did get a few orders too
for the old part of the school – Lupton's Tower, School Yard and
Upper School, before it was bombed, which gave her great pleasure.

The difficulty was that Dicky found it almost impossible to make
Chloe hear. Her high, musical voice didn't seem to get through to
Chloe at all, and they would often converse at cross purposes for
several minutes at a time. Oh, that I had had a tape recorder! This,
put at its simplest, is the sort of thing that went on all the time:

Dicky   Shall we have a cup of tea?
Chloe   No: we can't go to the sea till Sunday.
Dicky   (pouring out) It will be too hot for me; I like it cool.
Chloe   I like thittin' in the th-un. It warm'th my old bone-th. Oh!
           fank you, dear; what a lovely cup of tea!

When Dicky first came to us during the war she had the really very intelligent notion of being prepared, and when the siren blared, appeared at the bottom of the staircase from her third-floor bedroom, hatted, coated and booted, and hauling along a huge suitcase.

'What! Goin' out?' asked Chloe, from the depths of the oven. 'It's awfully dark and cold. And what are you luggin' that great case around for?'

'It's the siren,' fluted Dicky.

Chloe, who had the sketchiest of ideas as to how Dicky made her picture frames, responded: 'Oh! Couldn't you leave the wirin' until the mornin'? The siren may go off at any minute now and you'd loose all those paintin' fings.'

'I *said* "siren",' cried Dicky, almost in tears.

'You can't paint a siren in the black-out,' returned Chloe logically. 'You'd much better stay here and have supper wiv me.'

At this point Dicky gave up, and while with us never to my knowledge repeated the same line of action.

Sometimes they got so tied up that I had to intervene. Dicky, through dreamy other-worldliness, hardly ever took in Chloe's remarks first time round, and Chloe in any case could not hear her replies. They made perfect foils for each other. Chloe, with her black eyes and aquiline features, was imposing: Dicky was petite and slight with remarkably pale slate-blue eyes. Dicky dressed in pastel shades of blue and grey: Chloe would wear flame colour or adorn a dark frock with jade beads. I myself would wear anything I could lay my hands on that wasn't covered with flour or cake mixture. We must have made an odd trio!

Over several seasons we hardly ever became irritated with each other, which I think speaks a lot for all our characters, but I became very fond of this unassuming little person with so much talent.

Only once did Chloe exhibit exasperation at Dicky's eccentricities. This was when Dicky had come downstairs rather late to make herself some tea, but not so late that our customers had drifted away. Chloe had reappeared after her rest and was clearing up the middle room and I was charging between the gas oven and the washing up.

'Why don't you take your fings into the tea-room, dear?' suggested Chloe not looking up.

'All right,' agreed Dicky meekly, 'I can see I'm rather in the way.'

I also was too busy to witness her departure, or I might have prevented the storm. However, a short time after our customers left,

Chloe went to clear away. There she found our dearest lodger sitting in the window in full view of Eton High Street happily finishing her tea. This consisted of a piece of dry bread, an enormous lidless teapot belching steam, a cup without a saucer and the kitchen knife I was looking everywhere for to test if my cakes were cooked.

That our 'refined' teashop should be exposed to such ignomy was too much for Chloe. Dicky's soft little explanations that she thought we might want to use the proper china on other customers, that she *liked* cold tea and that she couldn't digest butter, went completely unheard or unheeded, and expostulations such as: 'Do you fink this place is a pull-up for car-men?' drifted back into the kitchen.

Having finished my stint, and being a moral coward by nature, I collected my coat and jauntily bade them goodbye, hoping things would have sorted themselves out by the time I came back. All was sweetness and light the next day, so I suppose they must have reached some sort of understanding.

I have explained that there were two rooms on each storey of the house. By the time you had dragged up thirty stairs to Dicky's room it was really very nice – well proportioned and adequately furnished, but I'm sorry to say we neglected upstairs shamefully. There was too much to do on the ground floor. Chloe, with her unruly heart, rarely ever got beyond the first flight now, where her sitting-room had become a bed-sitting-room. Until the time when we managed to get a second-hand porcelain one, the bath was unique in its dreadfulness. Chloe had once to fill in a form including a question as to how old the bath was. Her answer was 'antediluvian' and she heard no more! It consisted of an elegant galvanised iron tank, so huge that if you went to sleep in it you would surely have drowned. Originally it had been white without and within, but hot water and much use had caused the inside to become piebald, the surface partly paint and partly bare iron. It was mounted on four monstrous, claw-like legs, and although there were holes perforating the middle of the bath, at first I was completely at a loss as how to empty the thing.

'Oh!' explained Chloe. 'It's quite easy, really. You have to crawl round the back of the geyser and pull a string.'

I wish I had kept that bath as a museum piece, but the poor old thing had to be hacked to pieces before the plumber could get it down the stairs.

Once when I unwillingly went to springclean the spare room

against Dicky's imminent arrival I found a huge, multi-coloured mushroom-like growth emerging from the cornice.

'Isn't it pretty!' enthused Chloe, who had puffed her way upstairs to see it. 'Dicky might like to paint it!'

I pointed out that it Wasn't Healthy, and that she might not come at all unless we did something about it. Luckily Chloe saw sense and we got our landlord to attend to it.

Our landlord was the widow of a famous Eton cricket coach, a genial and much-beloved person, and they had lived in the house until he retired. That accounted for the mysterious brackets and hooks which stuck out over the landing and staircase walls, for these were where he laid his cricket bats to mature. They certainly added to the hazards of going upstairs. When we got ourselves or belongings hooked on the beastly things, as we often did, Chloe would always declare: 'That's ole Mrs Wright!' (Mr Wright had had two wives). 'She doesn't like this place bein' a teashop.'

When in due course we managed to get the brackets removed, Chloe transferred her slanderous accusations of poor Mrs Wright the First to hiding her favourite wooden spoon, or making her trip over something. Why this worthy woman, who had died over twenty years previously, should bother about us and our teashop I never understood, but Chloe rather fancied herself as a voyeuse.

This stemmed from her palmy days when she had joined a house party in an old moated grange and her friends had rather cruelly assigned her to the 'haunted' bedroom.

'I didn't know anyfing about it bein' haunted, dear, but I couldn't sleep a wink! Then, just as dawn was comin', I saw a figure of a girl in ridin' habit and carryin' a whip, sittin' on the edge of the bed.'

'What did you do?' I asked. 'Weren't you frightened?'

'Not exactly – I was startled, and couldn't move. I watched her until she faded with the increasin' light.'

I still don't know whether I believed her or not, but I know for certain that she sometimes displayed an uncanny sixth sense, though it couldn't at all times be trusted. Once she dreamed that she had won a football pool, and when a boy arrived with a telegram that morning she tore it open with abandon. She then found that the telegram was not addressed to her at all but to her current lodger, Miss Thunder (or 'Funder': I never found out) who was Not Pleased.

Anecdotes such as this would emerge when we went on our infrequent day-excursions to the sea. We seemed too distracted to have much consecutive conversation in the shop. Dicky occasionally came on these excursions too as, like 'Prinny', she believed in sea-bathing as a panacea for most ills.

One story, which Chloe told in the ringing tones of the deaf, convulsed the passengers of the coach in which we were travelling, though they tried to look as if they weren't listening.

'My pore ole Farver, bein' a married man y'know, was called in by the manager of the hotel he was stayin' at to try and dislodge a guest from a barf. She'd got stuck you see – suction!'

'Whatever did he do?' questioned Dicky, her pale eyes wide with apprehension.

'Oh, he told them to make a hole in the bottom of the barf, dear, and out she came like a cork.'

'How bright!' I exclaimed, laughing.

'Well,' said Chloe, warming to her subject, 'he wasn't really very clever, y'know – except wiv horses. And when he was in a rage he would rush up the stairs – all four storeys of vem in our house in Putney – and fling the maids' jugs and basins right down to the hall below. Most unnervin'!' . . . she paused . . . 'At least he didn't smash our better china that way, that was one consolation, and it relieved his feelin's enormously.'

'Were you fond of him?' I asked.

'No, he was horrid to my dear little Muvver you see; but all the cabbies loved him, and had crêpe tied to their whips on the day of his funeral,' she replied reminiscently.

Evidently Chloe's pore ole Farver was quite a chap!

*   *   *   *   *

'Let's go and visit ole Al,' suggested Chloe one early-closing day.

I had no idea who 'ole Al' was, but readily consented for it was lovely weather, and it was good for Chloe to have a change of scene when she felt like it. Nobody who has not worked in a tunnel-like kitchen for hours on end can appreciate the joy of air and sunlight to the full as we did. I had my daily ration in my bicycle rides from and to my mother's house each day, but Chloe, in bad weather, was sometimes closeted in the shop for days on end.

During the bus journey to Cookham – about six miles away – I probed a little as to who 'ole Al' was. As she was not referred to as '*dear* ole Al', I should have been warned. It transpired that her name was Alice, and that she had been a friend of Chloe's dear little Muvver.

Until she retired she had made a fair fortune in designing exclusive hats for the discerning in the West End of London.

The door of the comfortable-looking house was flung open by Al herself, a gruff, incredibly old lady, with straight, white, bobbed hair. Hovering behind was a dimly-seen form whom in the excitement of the moment I hardly noticed. Al seemed quite unsurprised to see us, though we hadn't let her know we were coming.

'Maggie!' she bellowed ferociously. 'Get the tea! We'll be on the veranda.' She turned to Chloe: 'Chloe,' she snapped accusingly, 'your father's name *was* Abraham wasn't it?'

'Yes,' replied Chloe.

'Well, he came through last night!'

'Oh!' said Chloe and seemed disinclined to proceed with the conversation. I was dying to know what 'Abraham' had said, but was too intimidated to enquire.

Tea was then brought to us by a 'real' uniformed maid (a rarity just after the war). She was not quite the same vintage as Al, but old enough to be bent and gnarled.

'How lucky you are to have a servant!' said I, as I munched excellent tomato sandwiches.

'Oh, you mean Maggie!' grated Al. 'She will have been with me sixty years in September.'

'She was wiv you when I came,' interjected Chloe surprisingly.

'Yes, and she served me better than you did,' growled Al scornfully.

I was bewildered, for insofar as an elderly lady of Chloe's looks and stature would allow, she resembled a chidden teenager.

Al gave a grim smile. 'As well as being my maid, she's my bodyguard! Didn't you see the papers last year? I was attacked, and Maggie saved me!'

I had to admit that I knew nothing about it, hardly liking to add that I hadn't known either of them existed until that morning. I don't think Chloe knew about it either, but she seemed to be behaving altogether very strangely that afternoon.

Maggie, apparently, was an East-ender whom Al had picked up from an orphanage all those years ago to run errands and make herself generally useful. In her gruff way Al had been good to Maggie, and after the rigours of the orphanage, Maggie thought herself in heaven. Though she never made hats, she had a cockney's quick wits, and over the years became a sort of P.A. to Al. When, some forty years later, Al sold the business, intending I think to bequeath Maggie to her successors, Maggie, defiantly obstinate, refused to budge from her side.

'You won't do no good without me,' she challenged. 'You can't cook!'

'Neither can you,' snapped Al, 'and I don't want a companion.'

'I can learn to cook, can't I?' retorted Maggie. 'And I don't want no companion neither.'

'I want a bit of peace,' growled Al.

'Yer won't get it if ye're ditherin' around the kitchen scratchin' for food,' replied Maggie adamantly. Then, changing her approach with native cunning, she added: 'I couldn't go on without yer, Miss.'

I got all this information from Maggie herself when I helped her wash-up, and left the two old ladies together.

Al, realising, I suppose, that a habit of forty years is not easily broken, and how useful Maggie could be in the house, at last relented. Maggie was to have the small bedroom, full control of the kitchen and her keep. Al was to be queen bee of the rest of the house and garden. Maggie, entering into the spirit of the thing, equipped herself with a cookery book, a blue print dress for the morning and a black one with a frilly apron for afternoons. Al deplored such 'ostentation' but on the whole this unlikely arrangement worked extremely well. Maggie always kept out of the way in her own territory when visitors were about, though this was no ordinary servant-mistress relationship. Indeed, when alone, I suspect that both of them enjoyed each other's company.

However, it was providential that when two young thugs appeared at the front door and threw pepper into Al's face, Maggie – as was her wont – was hovering in the background. Like lightning she seized the kitchen poker, shot past the spluttering Al, and gave one of the astonished youths such a whang that she knocked him unconscious. She then went in pursuit of the other assailant, who fled. Al, meanwhile, had recovered enough to telephone 999, and the end of the affair was that both ruffians were caught and eventually got a seven-year gaol sentence for attacking two defenceless old women. Defenceless, indeed!

On the way home I asked Chloe why she hadn't asked what her father had 'come through' for.

'Oh, *that's* what she said, was it? I was finkin' of somefing else and didn't take it in properly. She must have gone a bit spooky, mustn't she? Why didn't *you* ask her, dear?'

I said she rather frightened me, and that I hadn't liked to do so.

'Yes,' agreed Chloe. 'Even after all these years, she has the same effect on me. Of course I did behave badly to her!'

I asked her what she had done, and it emerged that when Chloe had been more than usually hard-up and living in London, she had asked if Al would take her on as a millinery apprentice. Presumbly in gratitude to Chloe's dear little Muvver, then defunct, but formerly one of her best customers, Al did so, and gave Chloe a thorough training. But it didn't work out. Either the hats Chloe made were so exquisite that she wore them herself, or they were so dull that she got bored with making them and didn't get them finished on time. Eventually Al sacked her, but surprisingly, never lost touch.

'She's a good business woman,' Chloe added reminiscently. 'She made me pay full price for the hats out of the pittance she paid me – even when I had taken all the time makin' them!'

I agreed that she wasn't a particularly lovable character and asked why Chloe kept up with her.

'Oh! Partly because I feel guilty about her even now, and partly she's become the only link with my dear little Muvver,' she replied.

*   *   *   *   *

The Fourth of June, the peak of Eton College's social year, was the only day in which we told the exact truth about tips, for, as I have said, we did employ helpers on that day and we divided the spoils among them. Chloe and I had, however, previously instituted a small comic money box on the tea-room mantelpiece labelled 'Staff' in large letters, which stayed there all the time. Naturally, there being no staff, Chloe and I benefited. It was not of course intended for use by our regulars, or the boys, but there were generous 'casuals' around who thought we might be offended by the odd twopence under the saucer (which of course we weren't), and who actually asked for it. At the end of the week we found it much more interesting to count than our routine takings, for we knew more or less what to expect from them. The most our tip box ever produced was eighteen shillings odd for the week, and I am sure that was because somebody put in two florins by mistake. We saved it up separately and in due course were able to buy some olde worlde oak candle brackets with which to beautify the tea-room.

'Well, we do tip the dustman and the postman at Christmas,' said Chloe one day, feeling guilty. I agreed, refraining to point out that by no stretch of imagination could they be labelled 'staff' anyway.

When the war was over, and the fireworks were reinstated, more often than not it was Grizel who gave us firework tickets. Throughout the war the Procession of Boats had continued, but Chloe *loved* fireworks. Actually they were something of an anachronism even then, for they were originally introduced to celebrate George III's birthday. Today, either through economy or the increased sophistication of the boys and their parents, they have been abolished. But to old stagers, like myself, as well as to Old Etonians, the Fourth seems to have lost a good deal of its glamour. Culminating as it did in mingling with the mighty for the Procession of Boats and the Fireworks, this day was the high spot of Chloe's year, and she wouldn't have missed it for anything. Footsore and weary though we were from a hectic, if lucrative, day, we would slowly proceed to Fellows' Eyot. It was important to get there in good time so as to spread our rugs near the river, both to see the fireworks reflected in the water and also to gain a vantage point from which Chloe could view the 'th-mart th-et' as they trickled in through the gateways. An early summer evening, the thump-thumping of a distant band, buzzing gnats, and the scent of meadowsweet and lilac always bring back to me the atmosphere of those Fourths. Much later, just before fireworks disappeared altogether, I sat with William on chairs on a dais among the VIPs because his grandson Fred was Captain of Boats. This was greatness indeed, and we were bursting with pride for Fred, but I couldn't resist feeling nostalgic for the long, uncomfortable, twilight-wait of the Chloe era.

Often we would have 'dear little Ivy', Chloe's dearly-loved sister, with us. Except for their similar stature they were poles apart in looks and temperament. As an ex-Indian Army mem-sahib, Ivy was always a little apprehensive of Chloe's public utterances, but despite this, she was very fond of her.

'Do you remember when we brought one of the bicycles up to the long mirror in our bedroom so that we could fit the skirt round the pedals?' reminisced Chloe. 'You weren't supposed to be able to see your knees workin' them in those days,' she explained to me.

'Don't you think that person over there in pink is charming?' Ivy hastily intervened, as she watched the ground filling up.

'Too best-y,' prounounced Chloe emphatically.

'What about the green one in the lacy hat?' I asked, knowing pretty well by this time what Chloe's tastes were.

'Yes, now I like that one,' she replied. 'That would suit you, dear.'

66

I told her I couldn't visualise myself cooking cakes in that outfit.

'Oh no, dear,' she exclaimed, horrified. 'I meant for Goodwood or somefing. I keep forgettin' about the beastly shop.'

She once saw Lady Diana Duff Cooper in the crowd, and to my surprise positively cringed. 'Oh, she mustn't see me now. I'm such a sight,' she moaned.

'We'll protect you,' I comforted. 'But why ever not?'

'I was her understudy for ages in *The Miracle*,' Chloe replied. 'But the wretched woman was never ill, so I never got my chance and was always in the chorus of nuns. Of course I had to practise just the same, and got a bit more money for that.'

'It was a spectacular C. B. Cochran show at Olympia,' murmured Ivy in my ear, 'About a statue of the Virgin Mary who came to life to take the place of a nun who had temporarily run away, I think.'

'Perhaps it was just as well I didn't have to be a th-tatue,' Chloe ruminated. 'I had awful catarrh thome of the time, and it would have ruined the thow if I'd th-neezed.'

'What an interesting thing to have done!' I exclaimed. 'Why didn't you say anything about it before?'

'Well, I rarver thought you'd look down on me for bein' "stagey".'

'What rot!' I retorted. 'I'm all the more proud of your versatility!'

Chloe bridled and was evidently pleased. 'I was one of Cochran's *Two Hundred Little Darlin's*, too,' she whispered, 'until Claud found out I should have to show my legs.'

'What's the matter with your legs?' I asked.

'Nuffin, really. But ladies weren't th-upposed to have vem in vose day-th,' she lisped.

Further conversation was cut short by the arrival of the Procession of Boats. Much has been written by Etonophiles about the procession, but I myself have always been somewhat vague as to its proper significance. Roughly speaking, boys who had reached a certain proficiency in rowing were awarded their 'Lower Boats'. Later, when they became more experienced, they were tested, and if considered good enough, were assigned their 'Upper Boats' and allowed to use sliding seats. Above all this, 'Captain of Boats' reigned supreme. He arranged the procession which consisted of both Lower and Upper Boats' boys, attired in what I think was Georgian sailors' apparel, manning a fleet of antique eights. These had to be manoeuvred in front of the dais, and at the psychological moment the crew had to stand up in the boat, Lower Boats with their oars aloft and Upper

Boats (because of the difficulty of dislodging the oars from the row-locks), entirely on their own. Particular interest was evinced in the crew of the craft *Monarch*. It was a curious old vessel, lovingly pre-served by the Eton boatmen, comprising ten seats and a cox. Top-ranking boys, such as Captain of the School, Captain of the XI, Cap-tain of the Boats, Captain of the Oppidans and so on, made up the crew, even if they were 'dry bobs' and had never touched an oar. The one concession was that Captain of Boats acted as stroke. They mostly made a motley spectacle when they stood, as their physique differed so enormously, but I don't think I ever saw any of them over-balance, such was the dignity of their high offices. A roar of derision met any unfortunate in the other boats who while trying to rise to his feet fell into the river.

The fireworks were really stupendous. Admittedly I haven't seen many other displays, but those I have seen bear no comparison to the Eton ones. From Fellows' Eyot, shadowy figures holding torches could be seen moving quietly on the opposite side of the water. There would be a squeal as an enormous rocket shot high into the air, then burst into a huge silver flower reflected in the river. Just as you were expecting the final silver petals to fade, there would be a second minor explosion and the sky would be filled with smaller pink flowers. Simi-larly, when the last pink stars faded they would burst into green sparks. Sometimes there would be as many as five different changes from one rocket. 'One, Two, Three, FOUR, FIVE!!' roared the crowd.

Then there would be the quiet ones which, after an initial tiny pop, seemed to fill the heavens with huge bunches of illuminated carrots. There was the coloured smoke which outlined the trees in gorgeous hues of red, silver and green. There were the little squiggly ones that jumped like dolphins on the water itself. There were the set pieces, the golden Niagara – a species of the familiar bonfire-night Golden Rain, but pouring from a height for minutes on end. There were the rather unpopular squealing fireworks that shot from side to side of a giant clothes-line. Then there was the immense reproduction of the Eton College crest, affixed to a twenty-four-foot-high gantry, the yel-low lion rampant and the white fleur-de-lis scintillating against a blue background and the whole mounted on the motto *Floreat Etona* in huge letters. Finally, there was a colossal set piece of the King and Queen, blue sparks blazing from the Queen's eyes; golden sparks from the King's and the whole outfit encircled with *God Save the King* in silver dazzle. Yes; definitely a fitting finale for a great occasion!

7
Coming-of-Age

The jaunts Chloe and I took together were perforce rather infrequent. First, I had to see that my long-suffering mother at home was comfortable. She had a dear, though rather silly, ancient retainer with her so she was never alone, and she was unselfish about the time I spent with Chloe. But she was becoming old and dozy, and I didn't like being away for too long. Then there was Claudie, that pampered cat to arrange for, and there was above all the spectre of about three hundred cakes to prepare either before or after our outing. These seemed to take on an evil character of their own when we wanted to get away. Either the oven became too hot for baking, or the cakes refused to cool in time for icing.

When at length we did get off, usually on a quiet day in the school holidays, our trip was fraught with hazards. Sometimes Chloe's crocky old heart began its 'trick-th', and I thought she would drop down dead any minute, or she would begin wheezing like a hearse-horse, which was hardly less alarming. Moving about in London was further complicated because although she would use an 'up' escalator, nothing on earth would induce her to step on a 'down' one. She insisted that she felt she would go to Hell. Bus steps at that time were impossible for stiff old legs to negotiate, so it was essential to have a working knowledge of which stations in central London had lifts. Once I made a hideous mistake at Waterloo and had to bribe the luggage porter to take us down in his baggage contraption.

Obviously Chloe's West End as she would call it, was very different from the swirling muddle it is today. Before 1914, for instance, she could recall driving in the dog-cart from Putney with her 'dear little Muvver' and choosing gloves at Dickins and Jones while the groom stayed with the horses until they were ready to return.

'That was where I used to live, dear,' she announced once, waving her umbrella, to the imminent danger of the rush-hour crowds. 'And there's Miss le Grand's flat, lookin' just the same. Her real name was Miss Large, you know, but she changed it to Miss le Grand for business purposes. She was one of *those* you know,' she added in a stentorian stage whisper.

Any doubts I may have harboured that she herself might have been at one time 'one of those' had long evaporated, particularly after the pathetic tale she once told me of seeing the most handsome man she had ever looked at while she frugally lunched alone at a fashionable restaurant, and hoped some of her friends would appear to augment her menu. She didn't have any luck that day, but every time she went to that restaurant, either alone or with friends, he seemed to be there 'lookin' out' for her. At length, on another lone visit, her admirer boldly strode to her table and got into conversation with her. He made a delightful and interesting companion, and what was more, he paid for her lunches for close on a week. Then, one day, according to Chloe, he turned his dazzling 'forget-me-not blue' eyes on her and asked her, 'Are you good?' to which Chloe, most reluctantly, replied: 'Yeth: I suppose so . . . And vat was the end of vat,' she sighed. 'I never saw him again.'

*   *   *   *   *

Incidents, some ludicrous, some painful, crowded in on us during our excursions. Once we virtuously attended a cookery demonstration. Ingredients were set out in orderly fashion on the table, including a large bowl of eggs; and would-be cooks or dedicated housewives strained forward to see and hear our slightly inaudible demonstrator. Chloe couldn't hear a word; but she *did* know about the unpredictability of post-war eggs. When the cookery expert carelessly broke three directly into her mixture without testing each one separately into a cup, this was too much for Chloe.

'Oh! How *rash!*' she exclaimed, in the ringing tones of one who through deafness did not know how loudly she was speaking.

All the room heard her, and what began with a slightly apprehensive titter from me, swelled into a wave of appreciative laughter from the rather bored audience. I don't think our instructor could have known what our hilarity was all about or from where it stemmed, for she looked very mystified. However, we did get a chance to explain and apologise, and it then transpired that all her eggs came daily from the organisation's Special Farm and there was no necessity to test for dud ones. Nevertheless, Chloe still thought she should have explained this phenomenon to her students.

A less fortunate episode happened once when we were looking round Harrods.

'Isn't she a *scream!*' giggled one of the assistants to me.

By some unhappy quirk, common I believe in many deaf people, Chloe heard her say this, and was mortally offended. It was only with difficulty I persuaded her not to go to the management and report the girl for insolence. But it was pitiful to see how such a little incident could deflate her so much. 'I suppose I *am* a funny ole fing now,' she whimpered.

'Not a bit of it,' I soothed. 'It's only the way you say things that makes people laugh, and even then they laugh *with* you not *at* you.'

She brightened a little, but it took a long time to mollify her.

Less eventful, though nonetheless enjoyable, were our occasional summer picnics in Windsor Forest with Kelly and Shaw. They held the virtue of spontaneity, and we returned home cool and relaxed rather than tired and exhausted. Kelly, by virtue of his being a chemist, was allowed a minuscule extra ration of petrol for delivering medicine to urgent cases. Like the true Scotsman he was, he zealously hoarded his ration, and when his store reached sufficient proportions, and his quota was due for replenishment, he cautiously used up the surplus on such excursions. Strictly speaking I suppose this was illegal, but we never went more than a few miles and I can't think of any four people who enjoyed such illegality more.

Paul Shaw had had to join the Navy when his age group came up about two years before the end of the war, and his C3 physique must have had something to do with his becoming a sick bay attendant. He had returned from the Far East looking a different man, stones heavier, with an authentic nautical roll and a seaman's twinkle in his gooseberry eye. But he had settled quite quickly and happily back into his old life.

Promptly at eight o'clock we would sally forth from our respective dungeon-like premises, Chloe and I carefully bearing our contribution to the treat – usually a baked custard made with *real* eggs, a large tin of fruit reserved for the occasion, and oddly enough, Heinz salad cream, which we seemed to be able to get wholesale, whereas it couldn't be bought locally. They generously would provide the first course of spam and salad as well as the drinks. There, under our favourite oak, we would begin laying the cloth. With exquisite courtesy a species of folding chaise-longue was set up for Chloe, who would collapse into it à la Madame Récamier (but with more clothes on), and in due course we all fell to our banquet. How pedestrian this must sound today to folk who are able to rush anywhere and eat anything they can pay for. But it wasn't like that then. Though we'd finished the Second World War, food was still scarce and unpalatable, and transport very unreliable. Hence, sitting in the summer twilight under our oak is a long-remembered pleasure.

A pleasure of a different variety was when Paul Shaw accidentally broke the neck off a bottle. He was a careful and conscientious man, and he rarely did this, but when it happened during the bottling of wine from his hogsheads, *I* was the happy recipient.

'I couldn't risk a splinter of glass being served to customers,' he would say, 'or to Chloe, but you and I don't matter.'

On reflection this was hardly a flattering remark! Nevertheless, I delightedly followed him into the tomb-like recesses of his bottling room where he carefully strained his breakage through muslin. I had the only stool and he sat on an upturned crate. Sometimes Kelly joined us and half an hour later the three of us would emerge much elated by the experience.

*   *   *   *   *

'Do you know somefing?' Chloe remarked unexpectedly one day. 'I've been in this dump twenty-one years!'

'Gracious!' I exclaimed. 'We ought to celebrate!'

'Let'th make an enormouth cake and give a free pieth to anyone who cometh in for coffee,' she suggested.

So that is what we began to do – rather to the detriment of our ordinary routine. Chloe managed to stay awake all that afternoon and direct operations, while I ran about and kitchen-maided for her. Luckily tea-trade was slack, and no Afternooners turned up that day. So while I found the largest cake tin to fit our oven and lined it, assembled the ingredients, cleaned the dried fruit, and so on, Chloe told me in more detail how the little business started.

'It was dear little Bébé who thought of it really. She had a house outside Maidenhead then, with a garden full of flowers,' began Chloe inconsequentially.

Of course I had often heard Chloe mention 'dear little Bébé,' but had not until then realised the tremendous role she had played in transforming the cricket-bat shop to the cosy little place it was. Bébé was a good deal younger than Chloe, but they had been friends for a very long time. She was well connected, and as girls they went together to the magnificent Edwardian house parties one reads about; notably to Solly Joel's the millionaire, to whom I believe Bébé was distantly related. They must have made a striking pair; Chloe tall and graceful with her blue-black hair, fair skin and dark luminous eyes, and petite, azure-eyed Bébé, her hair the colour of sun-scorched corn. Eventually Bébé married well and passed a little beyond Chloe's stoney-broke orbit. But she never forgot her old friend.

'Why on earth didn't you marry too?' I asked Chloe at this point, knowing full well she must have had plenty of chances.

'Well,' she replied, consideringly, 'I was engaged to Reggie in India for a lot of the time, and after that fell through, I never seemed to want to stick to the same person for long. They bored me after a bit, you see, though I liked their company . . . I had my last proposal when I was fifty-three,' she added reminiscently.

'And why didn't you accept that one?' I asked, thinking of the hours of work she seemed to prefer in her riper years to a comfortable retirement.

'Oh! I couldn't have done that!' she replied emphatically. 'It wouldn't have done at all! He was only about twenty-eight, and I'd got used to livin' on my own by then . . . Besides, there was dear ole Claud.'

'Why didn't you marry Claud then?' I pursued inquisitively.

'Well, he was always hard up, you know – lived on his bridge winnin's, he used to say. And of course he never asked me; but we did have some good times and maybe, if he hadn't died, we might have finished up togevver later on.'

She had previously told me that Claud had willed her such money as he possessed, but by some mysterious freak of law connected with family trusts, she never got it.

When she had got down to her last few hundred pounds, it was Bébé who suggested she should take a course in cake-making and set up shop somewhere. Bruges was Chloe's choice as a training ground since dear little Ivy had recently retired with her husband to Knocke-sur-Mer which was not far away.

Naturally Chloe made all the boobs – and more – that all novices do. Her best one was to bake a batch of eight large Madeira cakes and then discover that her dear little Muvver's diamond ring was missing. She was therefore obliged to buy all eight cakes in search of it

– to the almost total loss of her week's pocket money. But to her joy and relief she did find the ring in the seventh cake she cut in half.

Meanwhile, Bébé was looking round for suitable premises, though naturally she left the ultimate choice to Chloe. Bébé had not produced any family, and by this time had made quite a hobby of buying up and converting old property. She would live in it for a time, getting the garden shipshape, and then move on to the next house she fancied. All this experience stood Chloe in good stead when it came to setting up the teashop, though she sympathised with 'poor old Tommy' – Bébé's husband – who never seemed to have the same home for more than two consecutive years. Actually I don't think he minded so long as his wife and his comforts remained constant, and Bébé saw to that.

The indescribable muddle above-stairs had always puzzled me when comparing it with the pretty, welcoming tea-room. Chloe was artistic, as witness her dress sense, millinery exploits and the ideas she had for delicately decorating the cakes, but she was always hopelessly and unrepentently disorganised.

'Isn't it a pity I can't put fings away!' she would lament when she lost something.

Now I realised it was Bébé who (probably abetted and hindered by Chloe) had got the place to rights. It must have been she who arranged for the brass nosing on the step into the middle room so that no customer tripped during the whole of our time there. She it must have been who thought of the red window boxes in the front filled with geraniums. She too must have softened the harshness of the red and black fascia by lining the margins of the plate glass window with frilly curtaining, and it might even have been she who suggested hanging the blue witch ball in the middle which reflected contortedly Mr Kelly's shop across the road, and the passers-by.

'We had every table filled wiv friends on our opening day,' Chloe told me.

As there were only five tables in all that couldn't have been very difficult – but I am sure it was Bébé who arranged it. They had very sensibly opened just before the Fourth of June, and I must have been sweltering over doctors' accounts a few yards down the road, but I'm sorry to say the grand opening completely passed me by.

'Then, what do you think?' Chloe paused dramatically. 'Bébé went and found a house she wanted to alter hundreds of miles away, and we didn't have any flowers in the teashop for months and months!'

'Well,' I rebuked mildly, 'you couldn't expect her to stay in this district just to supply you with flowers.'

'No, I suppose not,' replied Chloe thoughtfully, 'though it was an awful blow at the time . . . but dear little Mrs Hartley came eventually, and she's a Godsend.'

By this time it was becoming late, but the 'enormouth' cake was ready for going into the oven.

'I'll bake it, dear,' volunteered Chloe, 'and then tomorrow when it's cold, we can finish it off.'

That is the worst of cakes. You can never finish them in one fell swoop. This one for instance had to be allowed to cool; then we had to cover it with almond icing and allow that to dry; then we had to apply the royal icing and let that dry, and finally it had to be decorated. I must admit that by the time we got to this stage I was pretty bored with our 'enormouth' cake.

'Let me finish it off,' pleaded Chloe, twinkling. 'You do the notice about gettin' a free piece.'

So I took myself off, and when next morning I let myself in I found that Chloe had protected her brain child from Claudie and mice with a monstrous dish cover. This must have survived from former days, and I suppose she had brought it down from the attic for I had not seen it before. Attached to the handle was a note for me: *Be prepared for a shock!*

Apprehensively I lifted the lid. There was the cake, beautifully iced in peaks all round, and on the flattened surface left for lettering, the old besom had artistically written in icing sugar:

IN MEMORY

of

21 YEARS' HARD LABOUR

It must have mystified many a passer-by when it was finally placed triumphantly under the witch ball in the window, but it provided a good deal of amusement for our regulars. Unfortunately the enormous cake was enormously popular for eating, so the joke didn't last long.

8
Flood and Fire

Things began to turn a little sour for us after that, but there were compensations. I have never known such a bitter winter. Everything seemed to freeze solid, including my hands to my bicycle handlebars, so that I had to walk between Eton and Windsor. Then Chloe caught a monumental cold which understandably developed into bronchitis. Almost at once my poor old mother in Windsor caught 'flu. Everyone was most helpful; snow was daily swept from our part of the pavement, and little delicacies constantly arrived for the invalids. This was particularly Christian, because if you gave away appetising little titbits in those days, you had to go without them yourself, for there was no hope of replacement.

Between the two old ladies and keeping the shop going, I nearly went mad. Of the two patients, Chloe was far the worse, for her heart began to be affected. On the other hand, my mother *was* my dear old mother, and accustomed to being cosseted when she wasn't well.

If it hadn't been for 'dear little Nurthe', Eton's indomitable District Nurse, I think I should have collapsed then and there. Edith Bodger, as she was called, can't be explained. She just was *good* – not churchy, though she and her family were enthusiastic churchgoers, but practical as well. Apart from being first-rate at her job, she had a great sense of fun, a lust for living and deep compassion for the helpless or ill. From nine o'clock onwards her spare little figure could be seen flitting around the little town, 'just bedding down some of my old dears' which meant rummaging out the right pills for one patient, filling the hot-water-bottle of another, straightening the bed or merely giving a word of cheer to another. This clearly was *caring*, and had nothing to do with her nursing curriculum. Nowadays her goodwill would either be paid for as overtime or she would be reported to her union as a blackleg. Luckily for us things were not all so regimental then.

Over the years she had developed a terrifying authority when she chose to use it. Once, the story goes, this diminutive person confronted a commercial traveller with delirium tremens. He had broken the pub's looking-glass and all the bedroom windows by the time she arrived and was beginning on the furniture. Quite understandably the publican and his wife were terrified. Nurse went up alone.

'Stop it!' she ordered quietly ... and he did! She then helped him to bed, gave him a calming potion of some sort, and peace supervened!

But she was not often like that. With Chloe, she had exactly the right touch. She treated her as if she were an ordinary friend on whom she had just dropped in for a quiet chat. Because of this, she did not inspire Chloe with the sense of doom that doctors and priests engendered. In good health or ailing, Chloe always went to bed very late, so Nurse would arrange that she was the last person to be visited. Often enough Nurse herself was almost asleep on her feet, and Chloe, wheezing happily, would revive her with hotted-up coffee from the day before. Nurse would then casually suggest simple and effective remedies for Chloe's ailments, and the local doctors trusted her judgment so much that if necessary they would produce a prescription for me to take over and get made up by Kelly, without even seeing Chloe. In fact Nurse was the only person who could get Chloe to go to bed. I could plead until I was black in the face that she would recover more quickly if she lay down and kept warm, but she obstinately maintained that she would feel worse cooped up away from us all upstairs in bed. Perhaps she was right, but she was a great anxiety.

My mother, contrariwise, and in the best Victorian tradition, was apt to make an Occasion of any ailment, however slight. Arrayed in her long-sleeved, frilly nightdress, her fleecy Shetland-wool 'fascinator' artistically draped round her little head, she would personify Woe. Her children unsympathetically called these manifestations 'Death-bed-scenes' and privately derided them. Now I realise if ever there was a candidate for anti-depressant drugs, she was one: but they hadn't then been invented. We had run through the whole gamut of local GPs, who began by being interested, but soon became understandably bored and unhelpful. Their considered opinion seemed to be that she was perfectly well and that she should pull herself together.

I now realise that she suffered from genuine bouts of melancholia, probably brought on by severe shock when my father died. My father, when I myself was just over two years old, said casually to my mother, 'Oh, I do feel ill!' sat down, and died ... just like that. So my helpless, Victorian little mother was left to cope with five children under the age of sixteen and very little money. She, who had never so much as written a cheque, managed magnificently. Gallantly she accepted the loneliness and responsibilities of widowhood, and adapted herself to the loss of prestige her altered circumstances brought about. The Imperial Service College which my father helped to found was in low water at the time, but gave her the lordly pension of £70 a year, and our schooling was greatly helped by my father having been a parson, for whom clergy orphan charities were available. But I see now that all these worries about money and bringing up the family must have taken their toll. I think she expected to join her husband in the grave much sooner than she did, but providence decreed otherwise, and she survived him by forty-four years. Now that I know what bereavement is like, I wish I had been more understanding and less brisk about these depressive illnesses of hers, which became more frequent with increasing age. This time she was at least stricken with mild 'flu as well, and that in itself lowers the spirits. But there she was, warm, lying at ease in her feather bed, with old Sal, the aged retainer, dancing attendance with hot-water bottles and other comforts. And there, one-and-a-half miles away, was Chloe, gasping for breath, slowly trying to rub rock-hard frozen margarine into flour to help me prepare the jam tarts. However, wasn't it Dogberry in *Much Ado about Nothing* who said 'Comparisons are odorous'? Both old ladies were very dear to me in their way.

One particular evening I was terribly fussed. My mother's temperature had gone up again and Chloe – who refused to have her temperature taken – had developed a hard little cough which could not be doing her old heart any good.

'I feel as if an elephant is sittin' on my chest,' she announced croakily.

Rather reluctantly, therefore, because Nurse was already overworked, I left a message with Hester (her cheery housekeeper sister) while I unwillingly walked home. Walking took much longer than bicycling, of course, but the frosty road was like a skating rink which made the bike difficult to manoeuvre.

At home, things were better than I expected. Mother's temperature was sub-normal and she was contentedly writing out instructions for her funeral. The next morning she even suggested sitting up in an armchair while old Sally straightened her bed – a great advance – so I naturally sallied forth in better spirits.

Arrived at the shop, I sprinted around in the usual way, getting ready for opening. I was a little surprised at seeing Claudie mewing around so early, for he usually remained curled up in his basket until the place had warmed up, but cats are always unpredictable, and I was too busy for my mind to dwell on it.

When the first few coffees had been served, I thought it time to find out how my aged partner fared. It would have been no use trying to see her earlier, as she always kept her bedroom door firmly bolted against intruders, and she was too deaf to hear me knocking. Instinctively avoiding the cricket-bat brackets and other obstacles set for the unwary, I slowly mounted our awful stairs. Claudie preceded me miaowing vociferously. As I reached the landing, a horrible smell became apparent. To my utter astonishment before me swung Chloe's bed-sitter door, wide open, and there was not a trace of her anywhere. Claudie, as if to emphasise my stupefaction, leapt on to her un-made bed and began licking himself vigorously. Idiotically I toiled up the forty-three stairs to the attic calling for her, but there was no response, and I knew she hadn't been that far for ages. I must admit that I then began to get distinctly alarmed. Then I recalled the horrible smell. One could see from the landing that her room was unoccupied, so I had not actually entered it. Her door was at one corner of the room and the fireplace was alongside it, so that part of the room was masked from view. As if to accentuate my concern, a flake of blackened paper floated out on to the landing.

I bounded through the door, and found not the charred carcase of Chloe which I had half-expected, but the ruin of her dear little Muvver's armchair, burned almost beyond recognition, the wooden fender reduced to charcoal, the hearthrug badly scorched, and a hole burnt in the floor boards. The fire, which must have been quite a blaze, was quite out and everything was sodden, damp and depressing. I was near to despair of ever discovering what had become of Chloe herself, when Claudie, having finished his ablutions, jumped off the bed, revealing a succinct note in Nurse's handwriting pinned to the pillow. *Don't worry! We have Chloe. See you later and explain.*

So my old friend was safe and sound somewhere! The constriction round my heart relaxed, and I flew downstairs to broadcast the news.

Hether happened to be the only one left, and he was just preparing to go. As he didn't even know that Chloe was missing, he didn't show a great deal of sympathy, but when I explained the fire, he became more interested, this being his concern.

'Now you'll be thankful I persuaded you to take out a fire insurance policy,' he grinned.

Of course! Hether was our agent. I had completely overlooked that aspect of the affair.

'We'll have to see how it started first, won't we?' I asked.

'Oh, you're sure to get compensation of some sort,' he replied. 'I'll bring in a form tomorrow and help you to fill it in. Probably you'll know more by then.'

Soon afterwards Nurse turned up trying to look penitent.

'We've got Chloe with us,' she explained. 'She's sitting up in bed looking like a queen, though she's got a temperature and a nasty wheeze. Now she's in my clutches I'm going to get the doctor to see her.'

'Thank goodness!' I exclaimed. 'She should have gone ages ago. But what on earth happened last night?'

'Well, roughly speaking, I set her on fire!'

'*You* set her on fire?' I echoed stupidly. 'What ever did you do that for?'

'Of course I didn't do it purposely!' she retorted astringently. 'It was really quite frightening while it lasted.'

I got most of the details from Hester later, as she is far less factual than Nurse, but apparently Nurse had returned home very late that night to find my message about Chloe waiting.

'I'll just run along while you're dishing supper,' she called to her sister. 'I won't be long.'

Nurse was one of the many who had a key to the shop, and there she found Chloe, eyes streaming, with hardly any voice, laboriously preparing a 'fly cemetery' (a species of mincemeat tart beloved by boys).

'I must finish this to help poor ole Peg,' she croaked, as she greeted Nurse.

'You won't be helping her if you have to go back to that hospital again,' returned Nurse with the authority of her profession. 'Now, leave those things alone – I'll tidy them up – and go to bed.'

'All right,' Chloe assented, her immediate capitulation giving Nurse some indication of how ill the old lady was feeling.

So between them they managed to struggle upstairs one step at a time. There weren't any banisters, so Chloe clung to the bat-brackets for leverage, and Nurse supported from behind. Nurse straightened the bed as Chloe regained her breath a little, switched on the electric kettle for a hot-water bottle and, sensing her fastidiousness about undressing in company, told her she would go and tidy up and get her a hot drink while she got into bed.

'Now, hurry up m'dear,' Nurse ordered briskly. 'It's cold up here.'

Returning in five minutes bearing hot milk, Nurse was astonished to see her patient, fully dressed, sitting on the top stair coughing painfully.

'Th-moke! Dear little Nurth,' she gasped, indicating her room.

Smoke was billowing out in clouds on to the landing. In a second Nurse somehow circumvented Chloe, dumped the milk into her hands and rushed to see what had happened. The answer was simple. Nurse, confused by the tangled mass of flexes emerging from Chloe's multi-plug had switched on an electric fire instead of connecting the kettle. The fire had been pushed against Chloe's dear little Muvver's armchair and its aged stuffing had ignited. Flame was licking up a flimsy Japanese screen (also of ancient vintage), and the wood fender and floor-boards were beginning to scorch. District Nurses are renowned for their presence of mind on all occasions, and our little Nurse was no exception. Promptly, with a mighty tug of the wires she managed to dislodge the multi-plug from its moorings, thus disconnecting the electric fire. She then poured the odd three pints of water with which she had filled the kettle on to the fender and floor – the area most likely to spread the blaze – and then looked wildly round for some container, other than the tiny kettle, with which to dowse the flames with water from the bathroom next door. The occasion was all too urgent for leapfrogging over Chloe again and obtaining a bucket from the kitchen. Through the smoke her eye lit on a large earthenware flowerpot holding a straggling plant. Instantly she pounced, and throwing the plant on the floor, rushed with the pot to the bath tap. She had of course overlooked the fact that this sort of pot contained a drainage hole at the base, but like the boy in the poem who saved the leaking dyke, she stuck her finger in the hole and struggled back and forth, back and forth, with this unlikely receptacle until the conflagration was nothing but a smouldering dump.

Only then was she able to turn her attention to Chloe, who, unlike

Nurse, was blue with cold and struggling to get breath. Nurse did not dare open a window in case it encouraged another flare, but now the emergency was somewhat abated, she had time to supply her patient with pillows, eiderdown, hot-water bottle and more drinks.

'Stay there!' she ordered unnecessarily.

'Can't move!' whispered Chloe chokingly.

'Won't be long,' comforted Nurse as she sped out into the street.

'Oh dear!' was all poor Chloe could muster, who must have thought she was being abandoned.

Within a few minutes Nurse was back again with help. How she managed to warn Hester and conjure a taxi from nowhere at that time of night remains a miracle, but like Sherlock Holmes, she had her methods. Probably the taxi-driver, like so many of the Eton towns-people, had reason to be grateful to her for some past kindness. Anyhow, by the time Nurse and the taxi-man had humped Chloe downstairs again and had driven the short distance to Nurse's home, Hester had a warm room and aired bed ready to receive her, and strangely enough Chloe ultimately seemed no worse for the adventure.

I don't know for certain, but I strongly suspect that Hester had turned out of her own room to accommodate Chloe and was sleeping on a sofa somewhere. I never understood the geography of their little establishment, but as well as Nurse herself, the two sisters housed and mostly supported an aged and slightly dragon-like aunt; so there couldn't have been much room. At any rate, after all this upset, exhausted Nurse returned to the scene of battle, made sure the fire was well and truly out, and tidied up generally, so that I shouldn't have any more work to do. Can you beat that for charitableness!

'Honestly!' Hester chuckled. 'My sister and Chloe looked like a couple of nigger minstrels when they finally got here! They were covered in smoke and grime, and you could only see the whites of their eyes.'

Those saintly sisters kept Chloe at their home for several weeks and I think that had she been looked after anywhere else she would not have got on to her distinctly tottery feet again. Indeed, it was difficult to believe how ill she actually was, because she was so happy there and interested in what went on. We all had to be a little circumspect about telling people, or she would have had a constant stream of enquirers, which would have disrupted the household even more than it had been already, as well as over-exciting the patient. I went as often as I could to see her, and sometimes took Claudie, but it was a busy time for me. Christmas was approaching and the Christmas cakes, though already made and maturing, had to be finished off. Fortunately my mother felt better and had begun trotting about doing her shopping as usual, which was a great relief.

*   *   *   *   *

Chloe's part-recovery culminated in a fortnight's convalescence in Rickmansworth with a charitable friend of the sisters, after which she insisted on returning home to assist 'pore ole Peg'. But alas, our troubles were not over. By this time it had stopped being so intensely cold, and the snow gave way to thick slush. The air became soft and balmy, but the ground was still so frozen solid that there was no means for the melted snow to flow away. Windsor is of course on a hill, but Eton itself is at river level, and on arriving one morning I was astonished to find Eton High Street emulating a miniature Venice. Water stretched from side to side of the road, though in the middle, because of its camber, it was only about eight inches deep. On the pavement outside our shop it rose just above the top of one's wellington boots. Gingerly I unlocked our door and stepped into the tea-room. I was greeted by a particularly recriminatory miaow from Claudie. There was not the slightest reason for him to worry. Certainly the tea-room was awash with about nine inches of flood water, and little paw marks showed where he had been playing 'shipwreck' on the polished tables. But thanks to the high surrounding wall of the backyard which we had always so detested, the water had not invaded our back quarters at all, and the middle room, kitchen and yard were bone dry. Likewise our wood block flooring never budged, whereas some College Houses afterwards had to have the whole ground floor relaid.

Much to the exultation of the boys, Trials, that is examinations, had to be scrapped, and they went home early. Something had happened to the sewage pumping station, and mostly because of that they had to go. That was another extraordinary phenomenon. Our aged loo, which was always going wrong, worked perfectly.

'There's somefing wrong with its balls,' I once heard Chloe explaining to an astonished plumber.

'Chloe, dear, you mustn't say "balls". It's rude,' I remonstrated. 'Its innards are called "ball-cocks".'

'That's ruder than ever,' she retaliated, unrepentant.

I must admit that in spite of missing a little of the boys' custom,

I enjoyed the floods. Of course the tea-room was unusable, but our orders for home-made cakes did not noticeably diminish. I still have the notice saying we were still able to make cakes, and any requests would be promptly dealt with if instructions were put into our letter box, which just cleared the racing torrent. Chloe too, thoroughly enjoyed the novelty of sitting at the first-floor window, her curls swathed in pale-blue chiffon, and letting down boxes of cakes on a string to her friends below. I had to open the front door occasionally, but was chary of doing this too often because more water would swoosh into the tea-room and might eventually flood our island of operations. Kelly was another individual who enjoyed the floods, at least after he and Paul had shifted the valuable wine barrels above water level.

Single line traffic through Eton High Street was the only way of getting through Windsor north to Slough and on to the Bath Road. Otherwise a detour of several miles was involved, motorways not having been built then. I think Kelly's shop must have coincided with a dip in the road, for every now and again the exhaust pipe of a car became filled with water which would bring it to a halt opposite his shop, and consequently hold up the long trail of moving traffic. Kelly, lurking behind in his murky dispensary would then splash out and give the offending vehicle an almighty shove, and this set the cavalcade going again. If I happened to be around I would help with this operation too, amid much bonhomie and backchat.

Another person who thoroughly enjoyed himself was William, my future husband. Released from having to mark Trials, he borrowed an old punt and spent a happy time punting stranded people, their pets and their belongings to safety. The balmy spring weather after that awful winter raised all our spirits. I think too that the comparatively recent Blitz had seasoned us to discomfort and loss of property, though undoubtedly hardship did exist.

For instance, my unfortunate friend Nell Kirk's pretty little villa in the lower part of Windsor was submerged in water to over the top of her gas cooker. She was obliged to remain there because her husband had severe 'flu, and was too sick to be moved. Somehow or other she divined that a neighbour, who lived in a bungalow, had panicked and fled, leaving behind her young lodger.

'Are you all right?' bawled Nell over the sound of the lapping water.

'Er! Not very,' came a faint reply. Dick was a bank clerk who possessed not only excellent manners but a surpassing gift of under-statement.

'I'll see to it,' shouted Nell. She was a little surprised that young Dick was unable to look after himself, but being a lady of resource, managed like a shipwrecked mariner to throw out a bottle containing a request for anyone with a boat to go and investigate. Late that day a punt did arrive and found poor Dick marooned on top of a cupboard, having broken his leg. He had expected the floods to diminish, not to rise, he explained, and did not wish to bother anyone.

'I'll look after him,' offered Nell from the window. 'I might just as well look after two invalids as one, but you'll have to get him here.'

The hospitals were full, so in due course the Red Cross sent a stretcher party, and after administering first aid, punted the securely trussed young man out into the flood and floated him half-way up Nell's stairs, where he was, so-to-speak, returned to terra firma.

'Is there anything we can bring you next time around?' asked the rescue party.

'Well, I'm rather short of fuel,' replied Nell, who had been doing such cooking as was needed on the minute bedroom fireplace. 'My coal cellar is drowned.'

'We'll attend to that,' they called reassuringly. Next day the much appreciated sackful of coal arrived, but rather to her dismay it was ferried by a brawny R.C. priest at one end of the vessel and a C. of E. one at the other.

'We're visiting the sick,' they called out cheerfully, 'and delivering goods at the same time.'

Neither of her patients were particularly devout young men, but Nell, being Nell, coped admirably. When the coal was safely stowed in the bathroom, they all had a convivial cup of tea, made with tinned milk, before these practical do-gooders punted off on their secular and spiritual visitations.

Following this Dick remained Nell's lodger for at least ten years, until in fact, he married.

In spite of such loss and discomfort, whenever I think of the floods now, I see in my mind the delight of one old woman. She had waded out thigh-deep into the contaminated water to rescue a long string of sausages floating about in the general mess.

'I'll give 'em a boil up,' she exulted, 'and that'll be the best meal my old dawg has had since the war.'

Clearing up, after the water had finally subsided is a thing I don't like to dwell on. Thanks to the backyard wall, which remained staunch throughout, I hadn't nearly as much to clean up as many others, but when Chloe for the tenth time remarked from the terra firma of the middle room: 'You shouldn't be doin' vat, dear,' I regrettably went up in a blue flame and suggested serving coffee on the sodden paper, manure and general sludge that remained. My outburst certainly shut Chloe up, but it was a nasty thing to do, because if her weary old heart had allowed, she would willingly have helped.

Before long, though, all was brightness and peace again. We had been given forms to fill in by the council estimating the amount of damage and the loss of trade we had sustained as a result of the floods. Because of the school holidays and because of being able to carry on our cake-making, our takings had varied very little from those of the previous year. Moreover, except for the cleaning up, we suffered no actual damage at all. This we duly noted on the form, claiming only a modest sum for the loss of our early-morning coffee customers (Hether and his friends), and for the odd candidate for tea. It was anyway too early in the year to expect much tea-trade. To our intense surprise the darling Urban District Council sent us a cheque for three times more than we asked for.

'Do you fink we ought to take it?' questioned Chloe.

'It must be a mistake!' I declared.

As usual, we consulted our mentor Ed Kelly. 'Och,' said he, 'take it and be thankful! I expect ye were the ones who put in the lowest claim, and they added some more in case ye changed your mind and came back on them for something more.'

He went on to tell us of some old reprobate he knew whom he had never seen wearing anything but dirty grey flannels and a pullover, and who had claimed an entire new wardrobe from the council. So after that we didn't feel so badly about it.

A few days later another official envelope arrived.

'It's an enormouth cheque from the insurance,' Chloe told me – and so it turned out to be. She couldn't possibly have seen the unopened contents of the envelope, so perhaps she did possess second sight. Nowadays the amount wouldn't have stretched far, but then it was riches. The insurance people had paid out generously even to the extent of giving us full value for a new armchair. Actually the sturdy timbers of dear little Muvver's Victorian armchair hadn't been affected, and with a little judicious re-stuffing by a professional upholsterer and a pretty loose cover, came to look as good as new. So what with one thing and another, we were 'in the money'.

'Let's go for a holiday, and let's give old Hevver some fudge,' were Chloe's simultaneous reactions. I heartily agreed with both these suggestions. After all, she had been awfully ill earlier in the year, and to tell the truth I wasn't feeling too good myself. As for Hether, he deserved bushels of fudge. It was completely out of character for either of us to be insured against anything, which of course spoke volumes for his persuasive powers as an insurance agent.

9
Final Fling

Arranging our six-day holiday was like organising a military operation. First, there was my mother to be considered. Sally wasn't really capable of taking full responsibility for her, especially if she got another attack of death-bed-scenes. So my dearly-loved and rarely-seen sister, Noly, invented some curtains that could only be manufactured on our mother's ancient sewing machine. Ma was immensely pleased and flattered, and almost indicated that I would be better out of the house while the great work was undertaken. Where ever Noly pushed her husband for those few days, I forget. All I remember is Ma's satisfaction, and my slight pique, at having Noly to herself.

At this stage friends and well-wishers tried to persuade Chloe and me to go our separate ways. 'It will be much more of a change if you each went on your own,' they said. 'Then you could swap experiences when you return.' It took a lot of argument to convince them that we *wanted to go together*. I suppose after eight or nine years that was rather extraordinary. As things turned out, how thankful I am that we stood firm.

The next difficulty to overcome was to arrange for the welfare and comfort of that pampered animal, Claudie. He had never been in kennels and I couldn't subject Noly to cat fights as well as possible death-bed-scenes, for our own domestic cat could be belligerent if roused. Eventually Mrs Hedley, mother of Olwen, the historian, a person of infinite compassion and sympathy with cats, agreed to keep him in their Grace and Favour house in Windsor Castle. Chloe maintained that after moving in such elevated surroundings Claudie gave himself airs when he came back and would not eat cod's head. Personally I think for a week or so afterwards he was too bloated with good living to consider any food at all worth eating!

All this had to be arranged in rather a hurry because we decided that we must be back as usual when the boys returned from holiday: so a few days later without compunction we pulled down the blind, locked up and sallied forth.

We had an ecstatic time! Nobody who has not been as hard-up as we had been, can imagine the glory of staying in a really first-class Brighton hotel, having the door swept open for us by ancient liveried retainers, and taking taxis everywhere. At first, admittedly, I felt like a sheep in wolf's clothing arrayed in the two-piece garment that Chloe insisted I should buy.

'You'd feel wrong in that fing,' she said, indicating my usual reach-me-downs. 'It doesn't matter how few clothes we have for such a short time, but they must be *good* lookin'.'

She herself looked (and was treated) like a duchess in a severe saxe-blue outfit adorned with a large half-moon diamond brooch, the stones of which were obviously real.

'Where on earth did you get that brooch from?' I asked.

'Oh! Haven't you seen it before?' she replied. 'It was my dear little Muvver's, and I always wear it on my vest. It's valuable, and I'd lose it if I didn't: but it'd be showin' off to wear it in the shop.'

I can't say our holiday was full of incident, but we savoured every minute of it. The glass-enclosed veranda overlooking the sea caught the spring sunshine and sheltered us from the wind. There we could watch the world go by, and Chloe could comment astringently on the current fashions. We ate delicious food with gusto, washed down with a carafe of wine, and we also enjoyed a stately drive or two along the front. Apparently this was the self-same front on which she used to sit with her dear little Muvver and try to concoct love letters to her fiancé Reggie, far away in India.

'I could never fink of how to put fings,' she lamented. 'And that was how it broke up, I'm afraid.'

Personally I don't think Reggie could have been suitable for her at all. I wish I had kept the few letters she wrote to me. They were always most graphic and descriptive: '*And there was Claudie, in his basket, with his hand over his face, tryin' not to inhale the fumes,*' she once wrote to me of a leaking gas pipe.

Sitting in a corner of our balcony, my mouth within six inches of her best ear, Chloe and I were able to conduct sustained conversation such as was almost impossible in the hurly-burly of the teashop. We talked about our respective childhoods at length. Chloe's was spent in those spacious days of the late Victorians. (Incidentally, she would always insist that we were both 'Edwardians': be that as it may, I subsequently discovered that there was forty years' difference in our ages, so that couldn't have been right!) In her family's huge house overlooking Putney Common, the cellars were full of wine, the stables full of horses. There were menservants and maidservants and 'darlin' Woggie' was taught by her 'pore ole dad' to drive a four-in-hand carriage.

My childhood could not have been more different. It was spent with my mother and the family in a Maida Vale flat, to which she had emigrated to keep down housekeeping costs while the older members did their various post-school trainings. It wasn't a bad flat, really, but it stank villainously of tenacious tom-cat which no amount of cleaning seemed able to eradicate. The hours of boredom spent in Paddington Recreation Ground nearby, or my tomboy antics around the coal cellars of Moorshead, Essendine and Wymering Mansions, did not at all match Chloe riding side-saddle in her beautifully-cut riding habit, drives in the company of her dear little Muvver, and later the dinners, soirées and garden parties she attended.

I did score one bull's-eye though, and that was when I mentioned casually that my mother and father had, in their palmy days before I was born, dined with Queen Victoria.

'You never told me that before!' cried Chloe, astonished and impressed.

The truth was I knew very little indeed about it. Poor mother, who was justly proud of the occasion, was never allowed to mention it by her loathsome family for fear of appearing to show off, so I was completely stumped for details. This seems a pity now, for there's nobody left who would know about it.

I heard too a lot more about Chloe's extensive family – most of whom by now seemed to have died.

'There was poor old Arfur: he was never right after bein' buried in a shell hole. Then poor old George fell down dead servin' a tennis ball,' she recounted, 'and Henry died hailin' a taxi. I hope I go that way.'

I observed that we were both past tennis, and after our 'splash' here, where the hotel porter ordered our taxis, we weren't likely to need any more.

'Don't be silly, dear,' she rejoined. 'I meant I didn't want to go lingerin' on and give you and little Nurth a lot of trouble.'

'You'd not do that anyway,' I comforted. 'You're pretty doddery now, you know, yet we get along all right.' You could say things like that to Chloe without her taking them amiss. Actually, seeing her in a different environment did emphasise to me how frail she now was, though still extraordinarily full of spirit. She chuckled as she moved off for her afternoon siesta.

In spite of the prophets of doom, our holiday was a huge success, and we returned much invigorated. It was just as well that we were, for a period of supreme melancholy now supervened. About three weeks before the news broke, Chloe's sixth sense began working.

'I know those men are goin',' she announced. She referred to Kelly and Shaw.

'Has anyone said anything?' I asked disbelievingly.

'No, but you see if I'm not right, dear.'

Unfortunately, she was quite right. They had decided to leave the rough and tumble of the Eton shop, give up the wine business, and settle in a prosperous little chemist's in the outskirts of Bournemouth prior to retiring for good. Kelly was approaching retiring age, and sensibly wished to get dug into a new environment before he did so. We both felt that part of our life was being wrenched from us. Though we were all too busy to see much of each other, Ed and Paul had always been our prop and stay where advice on business matters was concerned, as well as the main source of 'treats' and Christmas dinners for Chloe. Hard on the heels of this blow came another. Little Nurse told us that she would be giving up district nursing and was going to buy a nursing home in Windsor. She assured us that it wouldn't make the slightest difference to her nocturnal visits to her old friends in Eton, but after a time it inevitably did. People from miles around jostled to get their elderly relatives into this kind and inexpensive haven, and the nursing home became unspeakably busy. It was true that whenever called on, Little Nurse was always ready to come, but whereas you thought twice in the old days about asking her to do so, you thought three or four times now. Naturally enough, the new District Nurse did not meet with Chloe's approval, merely because she wasn't her Little Nurse, which made for further complications.

The worst bombshell of all was when I – even I – who had always been as strong as a horse, had to go into hospital for a major operation and be away from work for eight solid weeks.

'What on earth are we goin' to do?' sighed Chloe. 'I used to be able to cope all right, but I was ten years younger then.'

Fortunately I couldn't be admitted immediately. 'Oh! Something will turn up,' I responded, more cheerfully than I felt. 'It usually does with us, you know.'

But I was right. As soon as the gloomy news got around we were overwhelmed with offers of help and support from the most unlikely people, and gifts were showered on me almost as if I were going to be mummified in an Egyptian tomb. Indeed, when we had survived the initial shock, we began rather to enjoy the situation.

'What!' chuckled Chloe. 'Anuvver bed-jacket, dear! You'll be able to wear a different one every day you're there.'

Indubitably Eton snobbery exists, no one can deny that, but one should speak as one finds. Nowhere have I met such genuine sympathy, help or generosity as when Chloe and I were up against it.

Not unnaturally I was fussed about Chloe, fussed about my mother and fussed about the operation itself, though I think I was fairly successful in concealing my anxieties. Almost without our being aware of it, all these worries sorted themselves out. I caught members of our clientele saying to one another such things as: 'Well, I can't manage Mondays, but if you'll look in then, I could always spare an hour or two on Tuesdays, just to see she's all right.'

Mrs Johns, the bank manager's wife, volunteered to come in every afternoon while Chloe was resting and make my quota of cakes and serve teas. After years of knowing her, I only then discovered that before marriage she had been a teacher of domestic science. I'm glad I wasn't there to see her reaction to our topsy-turvy kitchen, but she coped manfully and efficiently for the whole time, bless her.

I had great hopes of getting my mother to go to a convalescent home during my absence, but not a bit of it. What would become of Sally all that time? And what would become of the cat? Here again the neighbours and the family banded together to see all went smoothly. In fact I think she had a whale of a time. I have now learned from experience that adversity in others brings out unbelievable virtues in friends and family alike.

I too had a whale of a time in hospital after the initial beastliness of the operation was over. This was followed by two weeks in a convalescent home specially endowed for 'women honestly endeavouring to earn their own living'. A book could be written about us 'honest women' endeavouring not to talk about our innards, which of course were the only things that interested us at that time. We were met with kindness everywhere, but I was glad to get away to the normality of the Attlees' home where they treated me like one of their own family – a great relief! They had retired to a comfortable house at Milford-on-Sea, and it was comical to see them cheerfully coping with household chores which at Eton had been performed by one of the five indoor servants. Certainly they had a nice old woman who came in the mornings to 'do the rough', but the once all-powerful Dr Attlee, sometime senior physician of King Edward VII Hospital, Windsor, doing the washing-up dressed in an old operating gown, and bringing round early-morning tea, seemed very odd indeed to me. He was still sufficiently convincing as a doctor though to insist that I should stay another week there, which of course upset all our careful arrangements, and must have been an awful bother to those at home; but they were compassionate, and the Eton/Windsor contingent agreed to forge ahead for another week without me, though I think they were rather tired of the situation. Nine weeks is an awfully long time.

I don't like to dwell on the first few months of return to the rough and tumble. I had never been properly ill before, and I suppose I expected to feel well at once. In actual fact I don't think I ever felt so miserable in my life. Added to this, my mother, who (thank goodness) had behaved herself with perfect decorum while I was away, had a superb death-bed-scene at the fishmonger's and had to be brought home in his fishy van. People as usual were immensely good and kind and urged rest: but I couldn't take their well-meant advice. Chloe had kept going marvellously, but looked like death and I'm sure my defection took a year or two from the length of her life.

Things were made gloomier some time later by poor old Chloe shooting from top to bottom of the first flight of stairs. She cut her lip and bruised her backside badly, though how she could have managed both injuries in the same operation puzzled us both. She also loosened her remaining teeth.

There was no room for a proper banister on those stairs – they were only twenty-five inches across – but following this nasty accident, we conceived a brilliant idea. We would have a rope threaded alongside the stairs on brackets, like outsize beads, bedded into the wall. The cricket bat brackets had fortunately by that time been taken down as being too lethal. Chloe insisted, however, that we must have nice pretty rope like they have in church. So I spent an interesting afternoon in Tufton Street, Westminster, all among church miscellanies of copes, crooks, stoles, kneelers, birettas and such like, and bought a dark red length of the woolly rope you usually employ for roping off pews. The etiolated assistant gaped a little at my measurements, but made no comment, and when it was fixed up neither Chloe nor I could think why we hadn't done it years before.

Toothwise, alas, the tumble downstairs was not nearly so easily resolved. I came to notice that my aged partner was living practically on slops. Little Nurse and I privily conferred.

'I think you ought to see the doctor about those teeth,' ventured Nurse on one of her noctural visits.

'Do you really fink so?' replied Chloe miserably. 'Why not a dentist?'

'Well,' replied Nurse judicially, 'after this fall your heart may not be behaving normally, and any good dentist would in any case send you first to a doctor. We'll go together m'dear. I'll make an appointment.'

Eventually, Chloe unwillingly, and after much prodding from us both, went with Nurse to see him. She came back with the news that Chloe must go into hospital for three days at least to have her mouth 'tidied up'. As well as the offending front teeth, the back ones were almost non-existent except for the roots and these too would have to be extracted to combat sepsis. Indeed it was a miracle, and thanks to Chloe's exceptional hygiene that her mouth was as healthy as it was. To her oft-repeated question, 'Will I die doctor?' he had replied sensibly.

'No you won't: not if you take my advice, that is.'

When I left Chloe in hospital I felt like a mother must feel leaving her child at its first prep. school. She looked so forlorn in her spotted sky-blue pyjamas and the matching chiffon bow at her neck for masking the wrinkles. The operation was fixed for late the following morning, so I left one of our long-suffering friends in charge of the shop, and hastened along to jolly up Chloe beforehand. To my relief and surprise she was in the best of spirits.

'What a *nice* doctor, dear!' she smiled. 'I asked him if I need divulge my age for his notes, and he just put down "over twenty-five".'

Obviously an intelligent house surgeon, I thought, who understood the vagaries of old ladies. He ought to go far!

'Stuck-up old thing!' I smiled fondly, and left feeling much happier.

Three days later she was back in the shop, new dentures already in situ, grinning from ear to ear and merely apologising for her rather slurred speech as she had to become accustomed to more 'teefe' than she had had for many a decade. Her gums must have been very sore and uncomfortable for a week or two, but we never heard a word about that.

Meanwhile a certain coolness had arisen between Chloe and Mr Johns next door, in spite of his wife having been such a tower of strength when I was *hors de combat*. Late one evening Chloe had practically blown herself up on the antique bathroom geyser, which went off with a terrific bang.

'And what do you fink Mr Johns did?' demanded Chloe wrathfully when I turned up next day. 'He just went to see if his beastly strong room was all right, and went back to bed! Someone might have been murderin' me.'

Apparently he also made disparaging remarks about 'The Silent Triumph' – which was the name embossed on the cistern of our ancient loo. He maintained that it leaked into the bank's premises. Up to the time it had functioned while everyone else's had ceased to work during the floods, we ourselves had grumbled like anything at it.

'Th-ilent Triumph,' Chloe would mutter. 'The beastly thing shakes the whole house.'

Now, however, since it had performed the miracle of keeping us in Eton and allowing us to go on working there instead of being evacuated, it was sacrosanct.

It was just as well that about then Mr Johns reached retiring age and the couple left Eton for Lancing, to be succeeded by the Gullivers, a much younger family with a nice small boy of eight. Cyril Gulliver, the new manager, was a handyman par excellence. What on earth possessed him to work his way up in a bank I can't think. On hearing about the Silent Triumph, he whipped upstairs, shuffled its innards about a little and asked for a piece of hosepipe. I can't say that the apparatus ever became silent, but it never leaked again. He was a wonder, that man, and the old place was never so free of squeaking doors, dripping taps, loose handles, unmanageable locks as in his reign. He even mended a hole in the oven door which we thought was wasting gas. His wife, Bay, often came in too, for she was lonely, and as a reserved Scot found making friends difficult at first. For me they rather made up for the loss we sustained when Kelly and Shaw left us. Not so for Chloe, I'm afraid. She had by this time become vilely deaf, and she became a bit jealous when I didn't bother to roar the odds at her, but mutter it in to Bay's receptive ear. They of course did not realise what fun Chloe could be if she was feeling well and

95

could hear what went on. Of course now it is too late I feel guilty about it.

* * * * *

Another Fourth of June was approaching, followed the next day by the Coronation of Queen Elizabeth II. There were a good many orders on the books for cakes, but these, to be fresh, had mostly to be cooked the previous day. One of our favourite boys came to explain that he wouldn't be needing so many scones this year, as he was giving his family sandwiches filled with mustard and cress which he was growing on his face flannel and sponge.

'What on earth are you washin' wiv?' Chloe enquired.

'Oh! Other things,' he replied evasively.

Before our annual offensive, I felt I'd like to go and see what the decorated streets of London looked like.

'If I were twenty years younger, I'd come too,' declared Chloe flopping into a chair. 'You must try and remember everyfing to tell me when you come back.'

I let myself in early the following morning, having stayed the night with a friend so that I could admire the illuminations when they were switched on. I was full of bounce.

I found Chloe sitting fully dressed with Claudie purring on her lap. She was quite dead. Like her brothers she had gone suddenly and quickly, but how I wish I had been with her.

* * * * *

That really is the end of the story of the teashop. I did manage to endure it for five months after her death, but all the gaiety and fun had evaporated with her passing, and it was a weary uphill struggle after that. The Dames, 'dear little Nurse', the customers, the Gullivers were all so kind and understanding that it seemed to add to the poignancy of it all and I was awash with emotion most of the time, when I should have been braced. On maturer reflection, I have come to realise it was the best exit the dear old thing could have made and what she had always hoped she would do. Life was becoming a burden to her, and she died in harness in her own little place and, as she would have declared, was carried out 'feet fir-tht'.